How to be a
Wine-Know

for the willing but uncertain wine explorer

by

Jennie Grubb

Ashford Press Publishing
Southampton
1987

Published by   Ashford Press Publishing 1987
                1 Church Road
                Shedfield
                Hampshire
                SO3 2HW

British Library Cataloguing in Publication Data

Grubb, Jennie
    How to be a wine-know
    1. Wine and winemaking — Anecdote, faetiae,
    satire, etc.
    I. Title
    641. 2' 2' 0207   TP 548

ISBN 1-85253-020-0

Designed and typeset by Jordan and Jordan, Fareham, Hampshire

Printed and bound in Spain by Mateu Cromo Artes Gráficas, Madrid

Contents

'At that price I thought I'd at least get a glassful'

Foreword

Like most young men I spent many an hour propping up a bar with a pint of beer in my hand. To be honest, I never really enjoyed the taste, but then, as now, the number of pints one could consume was a test of manhood. The difference is that today I'd be honest enough to admit that even the thought of a pint would be enough to make me throw up. I've flirted with whisky and vodka since those early introductions to alcohol, but now the spirits have flown from my booze rack, and these really are for me the days of wine and roses. And so, I suppose, I am now a fully confirmed wine-know.

My late father, a typical newspaperman, spent most of his leisure – and working – hours in pubs. He invested so much time in them he should have been a shareholder of Watneys. The consequence for me has been a total allergy to pubs. My perfect evening consists of good company, good food and some glasses of good wine. When friends comment on my expanding waistline, I'm quick to explain that a lot of money has gone into producing it.

One of my favourite restaurants in Berkshire has a wine list that's worth perusing if only because the prices leave you open mouthed. There a bottle of Chateau Margaux or Chateau Haut Brion or even a Mouton Rothschild will set you back a mere £1,250. Or how about a vintage bottle of Chateau Latour at £1,800? I usually settle for a bottle at around £15, and have often wondered if anyone ever asks for a £1,800 bottle. If so, is it a genuine wine connoisseur, or merely someone bent on impressing a girlfriend?

And how much would it work out at per glass, or even per sip?

As you'll discover in the pages of this fascinating book, more and more British people are becoming wine drinkers. It's good to see English wines becoming more popular and starting to compete with their continental counterparts.

As we become more and more a nation of wine drinkers, there is little shame in being a Wine Know. There's still the odd corner of these islands where it's looked on with a little mistrust. On a recent visit to South Wales, I was dragged kicking and screaming to a pub where I elicited some strange looks from the local beer-swilling rugby players when I asked for 'a glass of dry white wine'. Obviously, one of those Londoners not to be trusted!

But what is good wine ? Obviously, it varies from palate to palate. And so much rubbish is talked about wine. Like the man who sent a bottle back "because it came from the wrong side of the hill". And what did somebody mean by "too many tramlines" ?

There's nothing more boring than a wine snob, but most of us stumble through a wine list before settling for our usual bottle of Niersteiner or Piesporter. For many years I always ordered a Nuits St George because it was the only one I could pronounce.

Where do we go to for advice? Choosing wine is rather like sex. We've all spent too much time fumbling around in the dark. A book like this is long overdue. We all want to open our minds to new pleasures, but we need someone to point us in the right direction.

So, fellow wine-know, enjoy this full bodied lively consignment. I'm sure once you get your nose into it, you'll get the taste. For this surely is the Glass Guide to Wine.

Introduction

As a young housewife, keen and eager to please my new husband, I quickly learnt to cook; mother always told me 'It's face powder what gets 'em darling, but it's baking powder what keeps 'em!' This was fine advice and I progressed well, but I soon discovered that I was totally at a loss to know which wines to serve with these culinary delights. An Uncle's advice to me was 'Stick to Rosé dear, you can't go wrong, it goes with everything.' Well, I tried this, but besides most Rosé being a little too sweet for my taste, it soon became extremely boring. Like the 'chips with everything' syndrome, or the 'missionary' position only in bed, one needs variety to keep things interesting. There is no beverage with more variety and no subject more interesting than wine.

So how could I find out more? I found a couple of huge volumes at the local library, but...would I ever have the time to plough through them? Having moved straight from 'Mum's' to a new home, I wasn't used to ironing, cleaning, shopping, being a temptress at night, and doing a job. No, there had to be a simpler way to learn. What I required was a little book, explaining simply, all the things I needed to know. It wasn't available then, and I don't believe it is available now.

Eighteen years later, having found time over the years to study and enjoy wine thoroughly, I thought it would be a good idea to set these facts out to you. The housewife, newlyweds or live-ins, the young executive who needs to entertain for business, or pleasure, and above all, the man or woman in the street who wishes to treat the family every so often and know what they are serving when they do – all these people need advice. Families enjoy a special celebration from time to time, and what better accompaniment to good food can there be than wine?

It is not at all necessary to think only of luxury champagne-type wines, there is a huge choice open to you. My aim is to assist you in your enjoyment of these.

It is true that wine is an extremely complex and fascinating subject and there is certainly no shortage of written information about it. I shouldn't dream of criticising the truly excellent volumes available, in fact I list some suggested reading for those 'hooked' on the subject, at the back of the book. But for now I hope to dismiss some of the mystique and snobbery which can surround wine, and which can be so off-putting for 'beginners'. Wine is too much fun to warrant masses of heavy statistics – after all, what good is knowledge of how many hectares are planted with vines in France or how many gallons of red wine Italy exported in 1980, when you are gazing up at the blackboard in your local wine bar!

Wine is not, as some 'experts' would have you believe, a subject to be appreciated by the privileged few. Every year not only are people drinking more of this delightful beverage, but also, more people are discovering its delights. This is due to several factors including mail order outlets, and easier availability in the supermarkets and high street stores. The result is that in this country we have a wider choice than anywhere else in the world. Of course, when travelling abroad it is so lovely to try the local wines and we tend to remember the taste to enjoy them in our homes.

If you would like to know your way around wine, but are afraid to ask, this book is for you. By the time you have finished reading I want you to be able to walk into the oldest, and most established wine merchants with the courage of your convictions. Even if it is primarily to seek advice, you will feel confident that one or two aspects mentioned will be familiar to you. You will know:

- How to interpret the labels
- Where the different wine producing areas are
- How to pronounce the names of wines
- Wine words for different countries
- What to drink the wine out of
- Whether wines are sweet or dry

and much more!

Acknowledgements

To Jane for her encouragement
To Mr Alain Forsé for his excellent advice
To Sarah and Susan for deciphering my scribble

As a teacher friend said to me recently
'Unlike you Jennie your handwriting never did develop'

Part One

The Story

Noah putting his feet in one by one

A History Lesson

Though I don't wish to weigh you down with a multitude of heavy statistics, I think we should start with a brief history lesson. Speaking of multitudes may make you think of the Bible and this isn't a bad place to begin. Noah, when he landed his ark on Mount Ararat, promptly planted a vineyard on the nearest slopes (Genesis, IX, 20–21), and though this was pre-breathaliser times, he was in serious trouble with Jehovah for being drunk and in charge! This information from the chronology of Archbishop Ussher was a mere 50 generations after the creation. Archeologists unable to be as precise as the Archbishop have found evidence of wine-making some 12,000 years ago.

Entrepreneur Nebuchadnezzer, the Babylonian King, became an owner of vineyards and wine cellars, and there is a wine list dating back from that time in existence today.

The psalms of King David speak often of wine, psalm 104 vX says 'wine that maketh glad the heart of man'.

The Romans who, incidentally, were the first to acclimatise frost-proof vines, really used their famous noses as wine diviners when establishing their areas for planting. Starting with Rheims, the champagne capital, to

Bordeaux, famous for delicious red claret wine, and the valleys of the Rhône, the Marne and the Loire.

Though our Roman forebears may have shown great wisdom in finding the right areas for planting, they had failed to research France's packaging techniques and soon discovered that the French locals were not great potters, but as we know from their furniture they produce excellent carpenters and so emerged the 'cask' to replace the earthenware vessels previously used.

The vineyards were intensely cultivated and new vineyards established along the Mosel and Rhine in Germany, and in Hungary. Also, right here in England, the Doomsday Book records some 40 vineyards left by the Romans.

To begin with the Romans drank little wine, but in later years they became heavy drinkers which led to wine festivals – brawls and ultimately orgies!

There is a strong connection between wine and religion, when their empire collapsed, the Romans embraced Christianity and early Christian missionaries carried the vine further north into Europe. They needed sacramental wines, so quite sensibly wherever they built a church they planted a vineyard!

In Norman times, wine production and trade began to expand, the world production of wine was now in Western Europe, as it had long been realised that conditions in the Middle and Far East are not conducive to wine production.

Roman vineyards were legion

Roll out the barrel

In 1142 Henry Plantagenet married Eleanor of Aquitaine. Eleanor's dowry included large areas of wine producing country; Guyenne, Gascony, and the home of claret, Bordeaux. Not silly was our Henry, most men would have settled for a gal with her own wine bar!

Naturally, under the British Crown (where it remained until 1453) there was an ultimate easing of taxes, and during this period 'Claret' became the Englishman's staple drink. German wines also made their mark. In 1330 a gallon of claret cost 4d and a gallon of hock 8d.

As the French wines arrived, viticulture in England decreased and English vineyards were uprooted to make way for more profitable crops, although monastic vineyards survived until John Talbot, Earl of Shrewsbury, was defeated and killed at Castillion. Seizure of the English monasteries by Henry VIII lead to the abandonment of these vineyards.

With France now our enemy, imports from Spain and Portugal increased, Chianti also appeared on the scene, while from Germany and the Low Countries came Rhenish wine.

During the seventeenth century, deterioration in the quality of Italian wines and the heavy taxes on French wines brought a large increase in the imports of cheaper Portuguese wine. The signing in 1703 of the Methuen Treaty (a revival of the old Treaty of Windsor, which established Portugal as England's oldest ally), granted great commercial advantages and gave Portugal preferential duties on wine. Wise English wine merchants made their headquarters in Oporto, and Port as we know it today began to arrive.

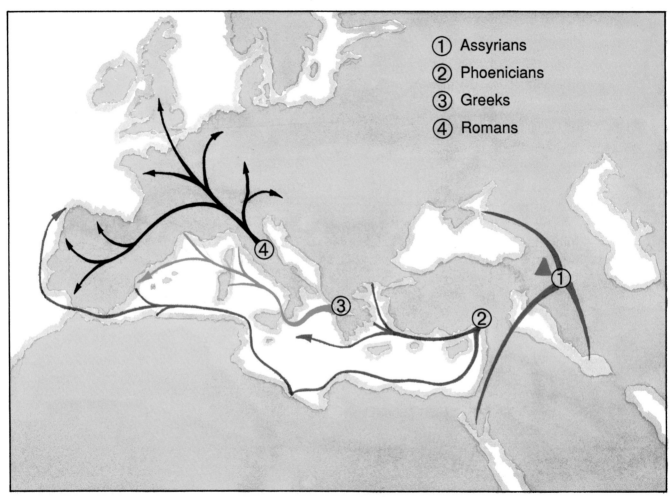

① Assyrians
② Phoenicians
③ Greeks
④ Romans

The origin and spread of winemaking

Portuguese wines accounted for two-thirds of British wine imports until late in the eighteenth century. Taxes on French wine rose high enough for people to seek alternative drinking habits. As taxes were paid on bulk purchases, spirits became better 'buy' because of their strength to bulk ratio. French brandy was popular, but gin received a boost when Francophile James II was displaced by William of Orange, and Holland Gin was introduced, which in its worst form even poorest could afford. Cheap English-made gin enabled the poverty-stricken masses to escape their misery and hardship into the oblivion of drunken haze.

The social conditions in England were appalling at the start of the nineteenth century but now reform was just around the corner. The growth of British Imperial power brought a greater and more diversified trade. Australian wines were imported. In the middle of the century French wines again become fashionable and claret was much in demand.

No matter how strong an effort was made to control its production and sale the lower classes remained faithful to cheap gin. Gladstone even reduced the taxes on light wines in an attempt to wean the lower classes off spirits. Later his government introduced much needed social reforms.

An attempt to introduce licensing laws failed in 1874 and in London riots ensued.

A customs official named Sikes implemented a sliding scale of duties on wines and spirits according to strength. A wine merchant of the day, fearing loss of business, maintained 'You can still drink Port lad, that's not ardent spirits' the port orders went up and soon became the Englishman's wine.

And on at last to the twentieth century. Port had remained all the rage since Gladstone's day until the late 1920s, and then became more associated with post-prandial drinking. Sherry became more acceptable for social drinking.

In 1949 Sir Stafford Cripps halved the duty on light wines bringing them within the reach of the ordinary man. In 1958 the duty on fortified wines was also reduced. However, the expansion in sales of the better classes of wine has been held back as successive governments have imposed heavier duties.

Not to worry, this wonderful habit of drinking wine is increasing. Every year is made easier as we taste new delights, and at home we constantly seek ' good buys' from the many outlets and mail order firms. We can raise our glass, and think of Pasteur, who wrote and campaigned about the health-giving qualities of wine. For the truth was, and still is, as many a Frenchman enjoying longevity will tell you, 'wine in moderation never did anyone any harm and many a great deal of good!'

Grape Expectations~the Vine

How to Grow the Grapes

Or, if you wish to sound knowledgeable, Viticulture.

Vine growing and the production of grapes relies on certain factors in order to be successful.

The Right Soil

Although the vine is grown in all sorts of soil, it is generally known to do better in poorer, stony and chalky soil, the reason being that stones and chalk are good for drainage and aeration. The stones at times act as a source of heat that radiates warmth. (Where the stones lie on the surface they reflect heat onto the grapes from underneath, unhindered by the vine leaves which protect their tops. This is the case in Chateauneuf du Pape.)

The Climate

The climate is also critical in wine production. A good balance of rain and heat is needed. A good spring to form the flowers, six or seven hours of sunshine during the summer months, a warm autumn to bring its grapes to maturity, and a cool winter to allow the vine to rest, but not so cold that the vines are frost damaged.

Vine growing is concentrated in two distinguishable belts. The main belt is the northern hemisphere, the most northernly area being AHR in West Germany, and the southern hemisphere as far south as Coonawarra in South Australia.

The Vineyard Year

Winter

We shall start here in the cold months, with plenty of tasks like ploughing to be done. The grower, or Vigneron, will hope it won't be brass monkey weather as severe frosts can cause damage to the vines, but it must be cold enough for the sap to withdraw from the canes for the vine to have its 'rest'. This is the time when pruning takes place, so no 'bleeding' will occur, and the quality of the vine will be maintained. All stakes and support wires are checked, and repaired or replaced. The vines are tied up to support wires. The vines are trained in various styles according to the region, climate, quality, quantity and soil. As all of you rose growers will understand, the ground will now enjoy plenty of good compost.

Spring

Early on serious pruning takes place. A second ploughing is needed to

Whiplash!

A snip in time saves wine!

aerate the soil, followed by raking between the vines. During budding excess buds and suckers growing below the graft area are removed. Frost is a great danger and might decide the quality of the vintage.

Summer

Weeding – as in all gardens weeds grow in profusion during the summer months. New shoots are tied up to the support wires. The shoots are trimmed to hold back growth. The vines are sprayed several times during this period. Summer pruning (excess leaves and shoots) must take place.

Autumn

At last it's time for 'The Harvest' (Les vandages or récolte) roughly 100 days after flowering, around September/October, traditionally a time for much hard work, but also great joviality. The right moment is crucial and a whole year's work will depend on the grower's judgement – it is vital to the wine's success.

The bunches of grapes are cut from the vines by curved knives or secateurs, and taken in bins or baskets to the press house and fermenting vats.

The charming sight of the peasant on his old oxcart will soon be a thing of the past, only to be seen in the masterpieces at the Louvres. In many vineyards nowadays machine harvesting is ousting the older methods. Once the grapes are on their way, usually taking a couple of weeks, the ditches are cleaned and the ploughing takes place. Also, to give protection against

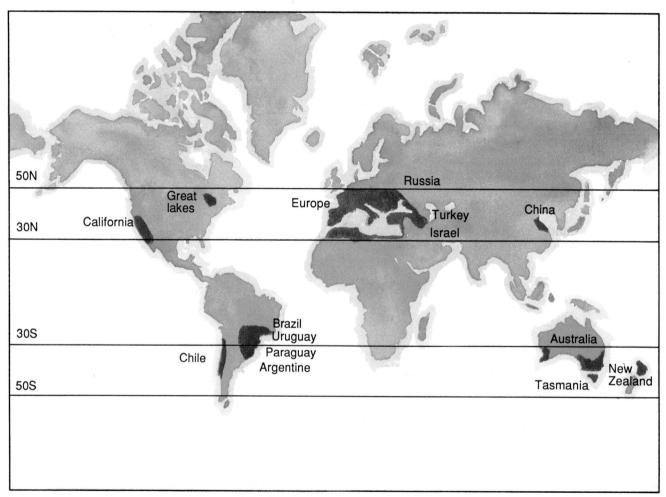

World wine producing zones

cold weather, it is necessary to cover up areas on last year's grafted vines.

Rather like roses, vines are propagated from rooting cuttings and grafting. The vine of prehistoric times was *Vitis Vinifera*, the wine bearing vine. It is, incidentally, of the same family (Ampelidacae) of another climber we all know, the Virginia Creeper. It is from *Vitis Vinifera* that all European varieties have evolved. Grown in different regions, processed in different ways, sometimes given a different name, it produces wines of differing characteristics.

There are several hundred, if not thousand, types of grape. Different conditions produce different results. For example, the wine made in Champagne from the pinot noir grape is quite different to that which is made from the very same grape in Alsace, Burgundy or Portugal. You may like to know the types of grapes used to produce the various wines. These we shall cover later.

In addition to the weather being kind, the grower needs to fight off pests and diseases. As well as mildew, black rot and odiumn, parasites such as choclis can destroy the fruit and the vine. Prevention and cure is the answer here, and most growers know all the modern methods available.

Somewhere between 1858 and 1862 a disease called *Phyloxera Vestatrix* arrived in Europe from North America. I mention this here because *Phyloxera* has a large part to play in the story of the vine. Within 20 years this almost invisible, louse-like aphid had caused havoc with European vineyards. This proved to be a great blow to wine production. By the end of the century most vineyards had to be dug up. Perish the thought – no vineyard – no wine! It is interesting to note how the eradication of the 'pest' was found. It proved necessary to uproot and burn the vine, then to sterilise the soil, but this was no long-term solution – the answer didn't lie as one well known gardener once said 'in the soil', it lay with the scientists.

The Yankie vine species, unlike the European vine, had developed an American immunity to the pest. Because it was not possible to plant the American vines in Europe and produce anything drinkable, the answer was to graft European 'scions' onto resistant American root stocks. This practice is now standard throughout the world. Unfortunately, the Phyloxera is hardy, and there is no absolute answer, so the world's growers will always be concerned. That is why, before replanting any vineyard, the soil is always dressed with strong insecticides. Once grafted the young plants are transferred to the vineyard at various stages. Like all plants they need carbon dioxide, light, heat, nutrients and minerals to do well, and will need a few more years before being at their best. If all this vine growing sounds pretty hazardous to you, you are right. Besides the need for the right soil, sun-growing methods and a slope, the Vigneron also needs a little bit of luck so that all factors culminate in an excellent vintage.

As we know, some years produce better vintages than others. A grower must take the rough with the smooth. After weathering bad growing conditions – a particularly scorching summer, or severe frosts – he can always partake of a couple of bottles from a previous 'good year' and console himself until the morrow!

③ *How Wine is Made*

How Do You Make It?

The principles of wine making, let's get it right, Viniculture or Vinification.

Wine is an entirely natural product, being made simply of the fermented juice of freshly gathered grapes. True, with modern techniques and chemistry a little twentieth-century 'help' may be allowed. However, the official definition according to the Wine and Spirit Association of Great Britian is that, 'Wine is the alcoholic beverage obtained from the juice of freshly gathered grapes, the fermentation taking place in the district of origin according to local tradition and practice.'

Now, local traditions and practice are likely to vary somewhat, like growing methods, from area to area, but in general, the basic principles are the same.

The yeasts, or ferments (organic cells which form on the outside of the grape) get to work on the sugar that is released from the grape as soon as it is crushed, breaking it down into alcohol and carbon dioxide – they in turn, are killed off by the alchohol they have produced.

The grapes are pressed in various ways, traditionally trodden by villagers, and nowadays by mechanical means. These presses de-stalk and crush the grapes.

When ripe, the grape will consist of about 75 per cent water and in the pulp and skins will be found sugars such as glucose, acids such as citric, malic, ascorbic, tartaric and tannin, esters and amino acids.

The grape pulp is then pumped into vats or cuves. Modern vats, like much of the apparatus used today, are made of stainless steel. Sometimes they are made of cement, then lined with tiles or glass. As I have explained, alcohol is produced by the action of the white 'dust', seen on the skins of the grape, attacking the sugars of the grape. These microscopic plants grow in the rich natural medium of the fresh juice and produce enzymes which convert the sugar, through an intricate series of biochemical reactions to alcohol. As we don't wish to be bothered with a lengthy explanation about molecules, in plain language this means:

Grape pulp yeasts (dust) + sugar = alcohol + carbon dioxide

This conversion, or correctly speaking, fermentation looks a little like your Great Granny on a Monday morning with her copper full of bubbling washing, except of course that copper cannot be used for fermenting wine.

The first step before fermentation can begin may be to add sulphur dioxide. This 'sulphuring' has two effects.

The juice of all grapes is white no matter what colour the skins. So far, the processes apply to all types of winemaking, but from here on it varies

20

according to the type of wine being made.

Wine Styles

Let's start with red wine – Cabernet Sauvignon, Pinot Noir and Gamay from the Beaujolais area are some of the important grape varieties to remember here.

During the vigorous bubbling process of fermentation the dark skins from the black grapes are left in contact with the juices in order that the maximum of colour can be extracted from the skins. What could be simpler, rather like leaving the red football socks in with a load of 'whites'!

I have, once or twice, been known to peel and pip a few grapes for special guests, because, as you know, although the flesh is moist and sugary, the skin can have a rather bitter taste, the taste of tannin, which is also present in the stalks. We all like seedless grapes because we do not experience the bitter oils the pips contain, a bitterness quite unacceptable in wine.

After about two weeks of seething fermentation, the young wine is separated from the floating residue of pips and skins (cap). This constitutes about 80 per cent of the liquid in the vat called the 'free run' wine and it is this Vin de Gouette which usually provides the best quality wines. The remaining liquid is known as Vin de Presse, usually darker and more harsh to taste. It is sometimes mixed with 'free run' wine to achieve a balanced

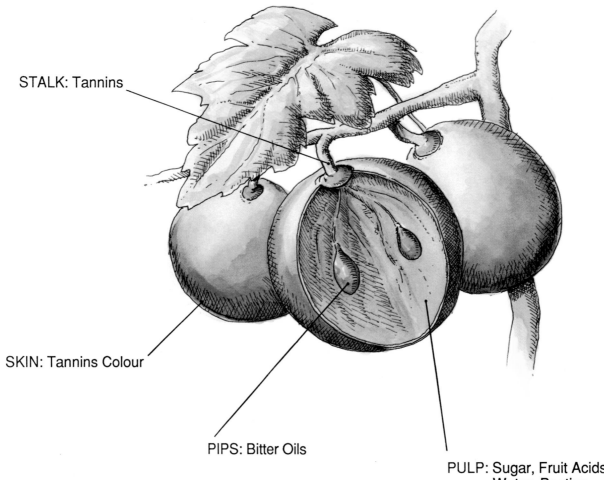

STALK: Tannins

SKIN: Tannins Colour

PIPS: Bitter Oils

PULP: Sugar, Fruit Acids, Water, Pectins

lower quality wine, and may be used as Vin Ordinaire for the vineyard workers. The residue of pulp and skins known as Marc is either used, in some areas, for distilling an outstanding eau de vie or will finish up on the ground as manure. Talk about waste not want not!

So far this all sounds quite simple, but there is a hazard in obtaining a proper balance between alcohol and sugar. The cask or vat the young wine is stored in must be scrupulously clean or, for example, one rotten stave in a cask can spoil the whole contents, as can one ginger nut in with the digestives taint the whole biscuit tin! He will need to protect his new wine at all times until it is safely bottled and stored.

In the wine, or must as it is called during fermentation, there is still a further fermentation to take place. The lightly bunged casks are allowed to stand for a year or more. Frequently they are topped up to compensate for evaporation. As the fermentation continues, the wine becomes lighter and less harsh as the tannin decreases. To obtain free wine from sediment (or lees) the clear wine is drained off or 'racked' several times into clean casks or vats.

I know it sounds like an old wives' tale but this 'racking' should take place when the wind is in the north, the weather is clear and the moon is full. There is good reason for this, for when such conditions prevail, it means that the atmospheric pressure is high and the wine will be less active, thus separating the wine from the lees will be easier. This wine is now said to be 'aged' and if it is to be sold as ordinary wine it may be bottled for sale or sold by the barrel. For quality wines, a further period of ageing, about a year, is required, usually in oak casks.

This wine will be racked several times and also put through a 'fining' process prior to bottling. The fining is done by introducing a substance that takes the impurities to the bottom of the barrel, like your plunger in the coffee pot taking the grouts down. It also helps to improve the flavour and stabilises the wine for longer keeping.

In the case of red wine the substance used by the vigneron may be beaten egg white, which attracts impurities in the wine itself, like bees to a honey pot. This suspended matter then falls to the bottom of the wine leaving it clear and in some wineries the wine is also filtered before being bottled. The process of ageing continues slowly in the bottle. How long a wine continues to 'improve' in the bottle depends on the type of wine. Some, such as the Beaujolais wines take only a few months to reach maturity, and may even spoil if left too long. Other red wines may still be improving half a century after they are laid down. However, only a very great wine will improve after 20 years, and will do extremely well if bottled in a magnum.

White Wines

White wine may be dry, medium or sweet – it is usually fresh and light in style. The grape varieties from which it has been made – Chardonnay, Riesling, Gewurtzraminer, Trebiano and so on – give the character of the resulting wine. White wine may be made from the juice of either red or white grapes, or even a blend of the two, because, as I say, the juice from all grapes is white, no matter what the colour of their skins, except for the 'Gamay à jus Rose'.

As with red wine, the first crushing of the grapes produces the best wine. Temperature plays an important part in modern wine making. Slow fermentation controlled by lowering the temperature of the big fermentation vats for instance, produces a finer white wine. Stopping fermentation may effect alcohol level and degrees of a wine.

Between a year and eighteen months in the barrel is usually sufficient before the wine is subjected to a fining process similar to that used in red wine. In many cases the sweeter white wines are passed through a heat pasteurization process prior to bottling, but the finer wines are rarely subjected to this.

Rosé Wines

The delicate pink colour of the rosé wines is obtained by leaving the skins of black grapes in contact with the must for a short period, depending on the colour of pink required.

Occasionally, a rosé may be dry and fairly high in alcohol, such as Tavel in the Rhône, but generally it is medium-dry or slightly sweet. Once described as 'good lawn-mowing wine', served well chilled, on a hot sticky afternoon, these young, light and delicate wines would be just the job.

Sparkling Wines

Well, we all know of champagne – coming only from a clearly defined and legally protected region of France – champagne is unique, but it is possible to make sparkling wine from all wine growing areas, simply by trapping in the wine the natural gas released by a second fermentation. Making champagne is a highly labour intensive method, there are other less expensive methods used and I shall explain this later.

Sparkling wines may be white or occasionally rosé or red.

Fortified Wines

Some wines have grape spirit (brandy) added during or after fermentation which brings the alcohol content up to half that of standard spirits. They are taxed more heavily, and the best known examples are sherry and port; others include Madeira, Marsala, and Vermouth, known as aromatised wines, and not forgetting the increasingly popular V.D.N. (Vin Doux Naturel) from Southern France.

Part Two

The Countries

General Terms

In order to gain confidence when dealing with this subject, it is a help to understand 'wine words'. It will also be of great benefit when you step off the plane, either for business or pleasure, for you to be able to order the 'style' of wine you require. I would never remember a great list at a back of a book so I have put these terms alongside the country, simply look them up when you've purchased your travel tickets!

Likewise, I have listed some pronunciations of wines you may come across in the future. One or two such as Château d'Yquem you may never taste, but at least you will know how to say their names! Some names will be applicable to both white and red wines. Before we go into 'countries' here are some standard terms used which will be useful to you.

Acetic	Tasting of vinegar
Acid	An important factor in the balance of wine
Astringency	The dry feeling produced in the mouth due to the tannin content, high in the younger wines.
Baked	A description sometimes applied to the bouquet of wines originating in hot countries, which taste earthy and cooked.
Big	Wine that's mouthfilling, full bodied, high in alcohol content and with plenty of flavour

I'm off – and so is the wine!

Body	The mouthfilling quantities of the wine
Bouquet	The smell of wine discovered by the nose
Dry	Self-explanatory in wine parlance, the opposite of sweet
Corky	A rotten persistent smell, due to a cork that has gone bad after poor storing
Earthy	Term used in wine tasting
Elegant	Decription of a fine wine
Esters	Compounds of organic acids and alcohols which give flavour to wine
Fat	Containing a high proportion of glycerine. A big soft wine
Fiery	Self explanatory wine term
Finesse	A wine term discription of how delicate the wine is
Finish	The after-taste characteristics – description of the length of time the flavour remains in the mouth
Flinty	Term used for slight flavour of gun flint. Due to soil content reacting on the grape
Fruity	Not meaning feeling passionate, a self-explanatory wine term
Full-bodied	High density of alcohol content and strength

Fat and happy

Grapey	The taste of what else – the grape
Lively	Describing the aroma of a good young wine
Maderised	Term for wine beginning to deteriorate and turn a brownish colour
Musty	Smell or taste resulting from maderisation, bad cork or barrel
Nutty	A self-explanatory term used to describe certain sherries
Oak	A taste which develops from the cask
Oxidised	A burnt raising smell, perhaps through faulty storage or exposure to the air
Petillant	Slightly sparkling
Robust	Full-bodied, rich in alcohol and tannin, may need ageing to become palatable
Spicy	A wine taste – for instance from the Gewurztraminer grapes
Stalky	Taste indicating the stalks got into the must
Supple	Subtle way of describing lack of tannin
Tannins	Substances occuring in the stalks, skin and pips of the grape tannins help to clear and preserve the wine besides influencing the colour

4 *France*

Understanding the Label

Since you often cannot try a wine until you have actually bought a bottle and drawn the cork, you buy not on taste, but on the information given on the label. Wines from different areas each have their own way of expressing the same facts. But recognise the basic formula and you have the key, virtually, to any label you will see. The colour of the wine, incidentally, is rarely stated, since this is visible even through tinted glass.

Certain facts, must, by law, be carried on any wine label; the country of origin of the wine, the quantity in the bottle or container (expressed in centilitres); the name and address of the responsible bottler or brand owner and, for EEC wines, the quality of the wine.

This is the bare minimum. Most labels tell you much more, such as the wine-making region; the vintage year, if any; possibly a sweet/dry description – this could be on a neck label, or coupled with serving suggestions on a back label – the alcohol content, expressed as a percentage, and the grape variety, if a single type predominates.

The vintage year.

The name of the property producing the wine.

Bottled in France.

Supérieur denotes a wine of slightly higher strength from the defined Bordeaux region.

Appellation Contrôlée provides the authenticity of the origin of the wine.

Name and address of the bottler.

1980

CHATEAU CHAUVIN

MISE EN BOUTEILLES EN FRANCE

BORDEAUX SUPERIEUR

75 cle

APPELLATION BORDEAUX SUPERIEUR CONTROLEE

PRODUCE OF FRANCE

BOTTLED BY LES CHAIS DU PRE LA REINE . 30300 FRANCE

The contents of the bottle in centilitres. The **e** denotes that the contents comply with E.E.C. regulations.

A typical French wine label

Description of ordinary table wine	Description of table wine from a particular region	Quality wine	Top quality wine
Vin de Table	Vin de Pays	VDQS (vin Délimité de qualité supérieure)	Appellation Contrôlée (for example, Appellation Médoc Contrôlée)

French Wine Words

Appellation Contrôlée
Controlled name – quality status

Château
A castle – in wine terms often meaning merely an estate

Commune
It is a small sub-division or Parish of a wine region – as legally defined

Cru
Used in France for vineyards of some importance, but literally means growth

Cru Classé
Officially recognised growth in claret making

Cuvée
A blend or content of blending vat

Faible	Weak or poor wine
Grand Vin	In the industry has no special significance, simply means Great Wine
Lie	Lees in the bottom of a cask or vat
Millésimé	Vintage
Mis (or Mise) en Bouteilles	Bottled
Mis en bouteilles au Château	Chateau bottled
Must	Juice from pressed grapes for fermentation
Négociant	The shipper
Négociant-Éléveur	Shipper and finisher of wine bought in bulk very young
Oenologist	Wine expert
Oenaphile	Wine lover
Propriétaire	Owner or proprietor
Pourriture Noble	'Noble Rot' or mould in over ripe grapes, which helps to produce magnificent sweet white wine
Récolte	Gathering of grapes.

Pronunciations

Carte des Vins *(Wine List)* Cart de Van

Vin Blanc *(White Wine)* Van Blon

Aligoté Ally gottay

Alsace Alsass

Barsac Baa-sack

Bâtard Montrachet Batard- monrachay

Blanc de Blancs Blon-de-blon

Blanc fumé Blon-fumay

Blanquette de Limoux Blonkette de lee moo

Chassagne-Montrachet Shassanne mon rashay

Muscadet Muss kaday

Pouilly Fuissé Poo yee Fweesay

Pouilly Fumé Poo yee Foo-may

Puligny Pooleen-yee

Quincy Cansee

Sancerre Son-sair

Sauternes So-tairn

Vin blanc cassis Van blon casseese

Vin de pays Vin de payee

Yquem Ee-kem

Vin Rouge (Red Wine) Van rooj

Aloxe Corton Aloss Kortaw

Beaujolais Bow-jo-lay

Beaune Bone

Beychevelle Bay-chevelle

Brouilly Brewye

Cahors Ca-ore

Chardonnay Shar-donnay

Châteauneuf du Pape Shatoh nurf do pape

Chinon Sheenon

Côte de Nuits Coat de Nwee

Côte d'Or Coat door

Côte Rôtie Coat Rotee

Gamay Ga-may

Gevry Chambertin Jevree Shambertan

Haut Brion Oh Breeon

Hermitage Ermitaje

Hospices de Beaune Osspeace de Bone

Julienas Yoolyay nass

Lafite La-feet

Latour Latture

Mâcon Makon

Mouton Cadet Mooton cady

Nuits St Georges Neww san Jorge

Passe tout Grains Pass too Gran

Pauillac Poyack

Pinot Peeno

Roussillon Roos-see-yon

Vosne Romanée Vone Romanay

Though other countries may produce more wine than France, it is an accepted fact that France produces the greatest wines, it has an unequalled range of quality and fine wines. Despite this, three-quarters of French wine produced is of ordinary standard, AC standard about 20 per cent and V.D.Q.S approximately 5 per cent.

Besides having a great wealth of tradition and practice, France exercises stringent quality control during the wine production.

Beautiful landscapes, idyllic villages and wonderful food are to be enjoyed in France's wine growing regions: Alsace, Burgundy, Bordeaux, Loire, Champagne, Rhône, Provence, Languedoc, Roussillon and Pyrénées.

These areas you can see by the way of the map. I'm sure you don't want to know how many kilometres long the areas are at this stage, I'll leave that for 'How to be a Wine-Know Extraordinaire'. If you are planning a hoilday and want to become more a Wine-Know, the *Wine Lovers Guide to France* listed at the back of the book has excellent routes, directions, wine festivals, along with some of the statistics I'm saving you from here.

Alsace

Curiously tucked away under the Vosges mountains, the Alsatian vineyards are probably amongst the most picturesque. On the German side of the mountains, the French side of the Rhine, Alsace has a varied history. It wasn't until after their liberation by the victory of the Allies in the 1914-18

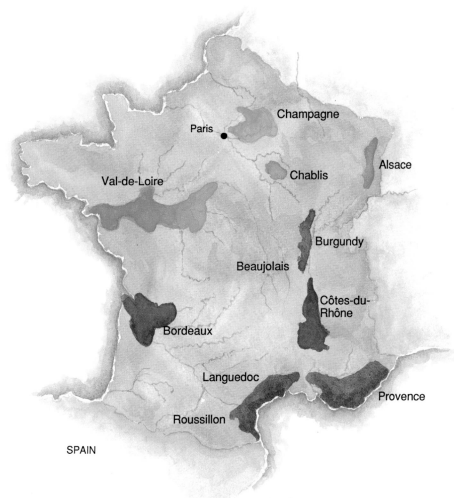

Wine growing areas in France

war against Germany that the Alsatians were free to concentrate their efforts on improving their wines, making them worthy of a reputation which the excellent position and soil of their vineyards made possible.

The small peasant proprietors generally belong to a co-operative society and seldom press their own grapes, selling them to larger estates or shipper merchants that own their own press houses.

The general custom is to name Alsatian wines by the grape from which they are made and not the places in which they are grown. 95% of wine produced here is white.

Gewurtztaminer

A distinctive spicy flavour, typically representative of Alsace wines. Like most wines of the area quite different to other wines produced in France.

Riesling

The best of Alsace grapes producing a delicious dry, crisp aromatic wine.

Sylvaner

A grape which produces a wine of great breeding, and makes a soft, dry, though less distinctive wine than the others of its class.

Other grape varieties are: the muscat, pinot blanc, and pinot gris, the latter known locally as Tokay d'Alsace. Look out here for the reputable shippers: Hugel, Trimbach, Preiss Zimmer and others, as you will seldom have a particular vineyard to identify; however, occasionally famous names such as Zahnacker at Ribeauville, Sporen at Riquewihr may be attached to the grape variety on the label.

A.C. Alsace 'Edelzwicker' is a wine produced as a result of 'blending' different grape varieties, although it is not necessary for the label to state which grape varieties have been used.

Alsace also produces an interesting semi-sparkling wine Crémant d'Alsace, which has Appellation Controlée status.

Burgundy or Bourgogne

Main Grapes – Pinot Noir and Gamay, Chardonnay and Aligote.

Burgundies are fruity and rounded with a powerful bouquet. Both the reds and the white are big, classic wines that often need lengthy maturing to bring them to their peak.

The range of wines here is second only to Bordeaux, but not according to a Bourguignon.

The red wines may possibly lack the delicacies of the clarets and are not quite so long lasting, but the mouthfilling qualities achieved more than compensate for this. The white wines account for a quarter of the wine produced here, both still and sparkling, and these are almost entirely dry in character.

The Burgundy region is long and narrow. Here you will come across names such as *Chablis, Beaune, Nuits St George, Macon, Mercury, Poully-Fuissé, Montrachet and Romanée.*

When selecting wine from Burgundy look for the following classifications:

- **Grand Cru** – which is applied to only the best vineyards of each village or even a parcel of land with its own name.
- **Premier Cru** – the next rank down which will show the name of their commune
- **Bourgogne** – the last rank and this is all this rank can call the wine, although it could possibly be from within some very good communes.

Travelling south east of Paris you will come across the first and most northern district of Burgundy known as *Chablis*. The area is devoted to and excels in the production of dry flinty wines with a remarkable freshness and flavour, the character being derived almost entirely from the Chardonnay grape used here. Watch the label, look for Grand Crû or Premier Crû, and essential for all Burgundies – Appellation Contrôlée.

The fine white Grand Crû wines can be enjoyed up to ten years or so, when with time it begins to take on a golden hue tinged with green, although most of the wines from this region are best enjoyed at about 2 years old.

The Côte d'Or

Chassagne, Montrachet, Puligny Montrachet, Meursault, Santenay, Volnay, Pommard, Aloxe Corton, Nuits St Georges, Chambolle Musigny, Gevrey Chambertin and of course Beaune are just some of the superstars of wine, and all rolled together in the heart of the quality vineyards of Burgundy. Here in the Côte d'Or, consisting of the Côtes de Nuits and the Côtes de Beaune you will find both red and white wines. From Côtes de Nuits comes Geverey Chambertin, Chambolle Musigny, Fixin, Nuits St Georges, and Clos Vougeot – big full rich wines which tend to be deep in colour. The vineyards surrounding the village of Vosne-Romanée produce the more expensive wines, but, due to heavy demand, even the second rank wines are highly sought after.

The red Burgundies of Nuits St Georges have all the typical characteristics of the big names, Volnay, Santenay, and Pommard which are from the Côtes de Beaune. Here in the famous town of Beaune is one of the most fascinating events from the wine calendar. A charitable institution, the Hospices de Beaune, is home and hospital for elderly people. The fine buildings which dominate the town were bequeathed a number of vineyards for their upkeep. Each year in November since 1443 a picturesque and festive public auction in the Market Hall takes place. Banquets, and wine tastings are held, traditions going back many centuries are conducted throughout the course of the weekend. Due to their charitable purpose, the prices fetched for the wines bearing their special label may be slightly exaggerated, however, the prices fetched by the various hospices' wines do give a guide to Burgundy prices in the following year.

Côtes de Beaune is home to some of the finest white wines of the Côte d'Or, and *Puligny Montrachet* and *Meursault* are names familiar throughout the world.

Aloxe-Corton, which is mainly red, is a name you may come across when buying. *Corton-Charlemagne* is one of the great wines produced in a vineyard from this area. A rare spicy taste which is quite memorable and has a character all of its own.

Maconnais and Chalonnais (known as Mercury Region) are home to another of the famous names of wine – *Pouilly Fuissé* (not to be confused with *Pouilly Fumé* from the Loire). This white wine, it is said, lacks the delicacy of Chablis and may be more subtle than the wines of the Côte d'Or. Representing good value for money the red and white *Mâcons* carry the hallmark of Burgundy – *Pouilly Vinzelles* and *St Véran* are names to watch for, if you enjoy dry white wines.

The small wine producing district of Chalonnais is responsible for both red and white wines, *Mercury* being one of the best and well known. *Rully* and *Givry* for the best reds and *Montagny* and *Rully* for sound whites.

Beaujolais

Beaujolais is the epitome of young, grapey red wine.

With Beaujolais *Nouveau* you can take the cork out and begin quaffing before the ink is dry on the importation forms. After a frantic rush to transport it, this straightforward young wine has all the wine bars and restaurants busy in November each year the day after its official release. Beaujolais *Nouveau* or *Primeur,* can be drunk without worry well past Christmas.

The Beaujolais produces as much as the rest of Burgundy put together. The climate is a degree more southern, and the land higher than the Côte d'Or.

The Gamay grape is almost extinct in the rest of Burgundy but does very well here on the granite soil.

With more than 60 villages able to call their wine Beaujolais, the system of classification is simpler and less sophisticated than elsewhere. It is necessary to ensure the wine reaches 9 per cent alcohol, 10 per cent will entitle it to the qualification of *Supérieur.* As the growers are much given to the use of sugar in the fermentation the required levels are not hard to achieve.

Fresh and Fruity

As a general rule the lower the temperature of the fermentation, the briefer

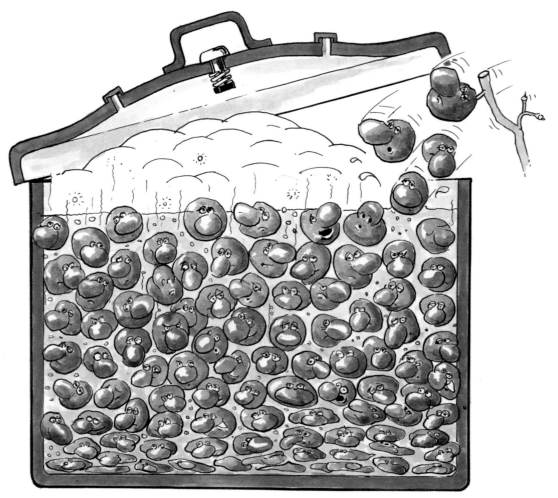

Hello, are you 'nouveau' here?

its duration, together with a short period prior to bottling, the fresher tasting the final wine will be.

To make wine which is specifically fresh-tasting you simply omit to crush the grapes before they go into the vat. The grapes begin to crush and ferment within themselves, creating a layer of carbon dioxide gas which sits on the surface of the vat and escapes, and effectively keeps out the air. As the process continues the grape skins burst and the juice carries on the fermentation. This process is known as 'macération carbonique'.

Top rank is occupied by *nine* villages.

From North to South

1. Saint-Amour
At the northern limit of the Beaujolais, neighbouring the Mâcon and Pouilly Fuissé vineyards, this is a small area (about 200 hectares) and produces a very light, fruity wine which can be drunk very young and cool, if you so wish.

2. Juliénas
A beautiful wine with a lively taste which it sometimes keeps for quite a long time. It can be kept almost as long as *Morgon*.

3. Chénas
A very small vineyard (200 hectares) bordering on Moulin à Vent. Generous wines with a distinctive bouquet, which sometimes attain the splendour of their neighbour.

4. Moulin à Vent

Along with Fleurie, the noblest of Beaujolais vintage wines; very powerful, with a full-bodied firmness, this wine can be kept for a long time.

5. Fleurie

Without a doubt, the finest of all the Beaujolais wines; very fruity. Although fine it is a robust wine with a close resemblance to *Moulin à Vent*.

6. Chiroubles

This highly distinguished wine is light, fresh, brisk, smooth, and very fruity. It is best when drunk young, as early as possible.

7. Morgon

The most robust of all Beaujolais wines; very firm and hard at first, it must be bottled after Easter, depending on the harvests, and aged for a year or so. The varied character of the soil yields a fairly large variety of *Morgon* wines. This is a wine which ages well.

8. Côte de Brouilly

A broad hill in the middle of the Brouilly area (200 hectares). This wine is more robust and long-lasting than:

9. Brouilly

These wines have more body and keeping qualities than the rest of Beaujolais. The smooth, sweetish, grapey flavour takes on new dimensions after some months in the bottle.

Bordeaux

Grapes – Cabernet Sauvignon, Cabernet Franc, Merlot, Sauvignon Blanc, Sémillon.

Types of Wine Produced

Sweet white wine, dry white wine and a few rosé are produced, but Bordeaux is probably best known for the fine reds known throughout the English speaking world as claret. This came about because during Medieval times when Bordeaux fell into English hands, the wine became an export commodity. Being a fussy lot, the Englishmen were adamant that no adulterated wine got into their consignments awaiting shipment. Elaborate steps were taken. This genuine wine became known as 'clairet' more as a reference to its colour because it was marvellously clear, and pale red in colour.

The word 'clairet' was soon transformed into 'claret' and has been referred to as such ever since.

The meticulous methods of wine-making continues in Bordeaux today. New wine is put into new barrels and is 'racked off', (transferred to new casks) several times to clear the wine. After a minimum of two years it is bottled in January or February when things are quiet; this is quite often undertaken by hand. These methods apply to high-quality 'Château wines'.

The Médoc

Making only red wines the Médoc is home to the most illustrious vineyards, and it has a system (dating from 1855) classifying the wines from the best Châteaux and calling them Grand Crû (great growths). These Grand Crû wines also command grand prices, and have indeed produced some fine clarets, *Latour*, *Mouton Rothschild*, *Margaux* and *Lafite*. There are, however, excellent wines to be found in the other classifications. Below the classed growths, first, second, third, fourth, and fifth are the Crû Bourgeois from the areas Pauillac, Margaux, St Estéphe and St Julien which produce a wine with a good reputation, representing good value for money and of a high standard.

An inexperienced wine drinker will enjoy, I'm sure, comparing the wines from this region as they are easily available. The wine will be light in colour, dry and refreshing; although when too young the wine can give the impression of being harsh, but it will always improve with age. Margaux in the southern Médoc is known for its delicacy and perfume, the fruitiness and scent are enhanced by the brilliant colour of Pauillac whilst St Estéphe produces a 'bigger' and 'stronger' flavoured wine.

Pomerol and **St Emilion** (classified in 1955) like the Médoc produce only red wine, but they are generally softer and gentler. Full of flavour, these wines produce the balance of mature wine early, developing a round rich softness.

The famous **Château Pétrus** is one of the finest in Pomerol, although one of the most costly. Darker than most Bordeaux wines, Pomerol's rich smooth and satisfying characteristics make them very easy drinking. Merlot, a grape not used so much in the rest of the Bordeaux region is the main grape variety.

St Emilion whose wines are rich, rounded and amenable also has Merlot as the chief grape variety. Château Cheval Blanc is St Emilon's top vineyard and wine.

Graves is associated with white wine and this accounts for half its production, although the red can hold its head up well against the best of Médoc. Some of the names you may come across are the greatest Graves, *Château Haut-Brion* (classified in 1855) and the *Domaine de Chevalier*.

Sauternes and **Barsac** produce only white wine. This small district is encircled by Graves but this white wine has an *amazing difference*. The grapes are left on the vine long after the date of harvest. When under ideal conditions, a fungus will form on the skins and dehydrate the grapes thus concentrating the sugar. The shrivelled grapes with their sugary juice are then made into the rich dessert wine of Sauternes. The rotting grape process is called in French 'Pourriture Noble' or noble rot. This process is not unique, in Germany it is known as 'Edelfäule', in Italy, 'Muffa Nobile', with *Picolit* as the most famous; in Austria it gives 'Ausbruch' wines their

A load of rot

sweetness and in Hungary it is known as 'Aszu' and gives *Tokay Eszencia* and *Aszu*. This process is also used in other parts of the world, particularly California.

This delicious honey-like nectar of Sauternes has among its Châteaux a wine in a class of its own, the infamous *Château d'Yquem*, followed by 11 first growths and 12 seconds.

As you may imagine, this rotting of the grapes is a risky business, the quality depends heavily on ideal weather conditions and the ability of the grower to leave the grape as long as possible. Some of the smaller vineyards cannot afford the gamble in the risky October weather and pick a little early, consequently there is a world of difference between the Great Châteaux and the lesser ones.

Good value is an important factor in buying anything and can be found in these Bordeaux bargains:

Entre Deux Mers (between two seas) is a vast area, lying between two rivers, the Gironde and the Garonne, that produces a dryish white wine of consistent, if not remarkable, quality. The wine is easily available at a sensible price. A strip of land on the east bank of the Garonne produces a red and white wine, usually reasonably priced, known as the *Premières Côtes de Bordeaux* (sweet white).

Bergerac – This A.C. region is smaller than Bordeaux and produces some good red and white wines. The grapes used here are mostly Cabernet and Merlot for the reds. The A.C. district of Pécharmant has a light red wine made mainly from the Malbec grape.

One must mention here *Montbazillac*, an elegant sweet white wine from the Muscat grape. Therefore it is no surprise it bears some similarities to the wines of Sauternes, and is an excellent alternative when looking for value for money.

Cerons – close to the river Garonne and adjacent to Sauternes. The wines from Loupiac, Ste Croix du Mont and Cérons are less expensive than their neighbours but at times are inclined to be rich and sweet.

Fronsac, Bourg and Blaye are generally considered to produce wine of lesser quality than the 'Great' claret-making districts. This may be fair comment but these three areas on the north-east bank of the Dordogne produce some everyday drinking wines that are good, and can sometimes certainly provide some genuine bargains.

"Champagne"

Grapes – Pinot Noir, Pinot Meunier and Chardonnay

Think of Champagne and you'll think of parties, style, sophistication, elegance and dare I say it, expense. However, Champagne is not a mere sparkling wine. It is painstakingly prepared in accordance with precise rules and disciplines from knowledge acquired over many years. Don Perignon, a monk and head cellarman at the Benedictine Abbey of Hautvilliers was the inventor of Champagne, at the beginning of the eighteenth century.

Champagne comes from a closely defined area, 90 miles east of Paris, the commercial areas being Rheims and Epernay. The countryside is gently rolling with a unique, deep chalky soil, and grows both black and white grapes which are both used in its making.

Every Champagne is a blend of the most suitable characteristics of different vineyards of the region, obtaining a perfectly well-balanced wine.

More often than not, a certain amount of wine reserved from previous years is incorporated in the blend, making it 'Non-Vintage (N-V) Champagne'. However, if it is the product of a particular year with exceptional qualities or characteristics, no addition is made to it and it then becomes a 'Vintage Champagne'.

The Birth of the Bubble

After the blending of the wine, the wine has a small legal quantity of cane

Great delivery but what about the bill?

sugar added to it, and is then bottled to ferment a second time, for 3–5 months.

The sugar is transformed into alcohol and carbonic gas, which stays enclosed in the bottle, and which when the bottle is uncorked, will give the wine it's 'head'.

This second fermentation causes a deposit to form in the bottle that has to be removed. Now I find this next process unbelievable, but it works. The bottles are placed neck first, horizontally in racks with a hole for each bottle. Skilled workers, or sometimes nowadays machines, shake and tilt each bottle upwards 'every day' for several weeks (up to 3 months). This operation is known as 'Remuage'. In this way deposits slowly collect and adhere to the cork. Then a chap, or a machine called a Dégorgeur, removes the cork with the deposit, about 5 cm or 2 in. of wine, by freezing the neck of the bottle, removing the cork and allowing the pressure of the wine to shoot out the frozen solid plug of sediment. The bottle is then topped up with a mixture of sugar and wine (Dosage) – in practice even the driest wines are very slightly sweetened. The process is critical to the style of the wine, adjusting the taste to suit the various market requirements.

Brut	Very Dry
Extra Sec – Trés Sec	Dry
Sec	Medium Dry
Demi Sec	Medium Sweet
Rich	Sweet

Let's not forget 1 year is compulsory for maturation, 3 years for vintage and overall a good 2 years' work to produce one non-vintage bottle.

The Champagne then receives its final cork and is 'dressed up' ready for despatch. Until the EEC decided for reasons best known to themselves, to ban the term, this was called 'Méthode Champenoise'.

Now you know why it has acquired a unique and unequalled reputation and why other products seek and try to imitate it. There is only one champagne, that is what you want if you require that extra bubble.

Having said that, it is a good idea to know of the other 'fizzy' wines available which are truly excellent but are made by quite different methods.

Firstly, the 'tank' method (or cuvé closé or charmat).

Early in the nineteenth century, it was suggested that to avoid all the bottle shaking (remuage) and removal of the sediment (dégorgement), that the second bubble-producing fermentation could be carried out in a 'tank'. This is certainly successful and many excellent sparkling wines are produced in this way. It is a good deal cheaper to produce sparkling wine in this way, but the product doesn't quite have the same 'fizz' ; the sparkle is 'that of Brighton rather than Bath'.

Large enamelled steel tanks are used after fermentation is exhausted; the wine settles prior to being filtered (under pressure) into another tank, from which it is bottled. The 'dosage', sugar usually mixed with brandy, is added either to empty bottles or to the 'tank'.

The world annual production of sparkling wine runs into millions of bottles, and that is not including Champagne. One of the most popular sparkling wines here in Britain is the Italian *Asti*, followed closely by the French and, though of excellent quality, German *Sekt* trails surprisingly behind. The other method of putting bubbles into 'fizzies' is the Impregnation Method, or Pompe Bicyclette.

Even less costly than Champagne production or the tank method, this is the method by which sparkling wines are made by cooling a suitable wine, then under low pressure forcing carbon dioxide into it. The sparkle of these wines quickly disappears in the glass – 'the sparkle of Bognor rather than Brighton'!

Sparkling Words

Blanc de blancs White wine made exclusively from white grapes.

Blanc de noirs White wine made from black grapes.

Champagne Under European Law, only wine made by the Champagne region of north-east France can *properly* be called champagne. But also Canada, California and Australia have the right to enjoy the privilege.

Crémant Sparkling wine with slightly less fizz (3.5 to 4.5 atmospheres against 5.6 for champagne). Confusingly, though Crémant d'Alsace is as fizzy as champagne.

Full of wind!

A.C. Côteaux Champenois	White and red *non*-sparkling wine from Champagne.
Pink Champagne	Increasingly popular again. It is made by adding red wine to the blend before second fermentation.

As it seems to be a question on all the television quiz shows, here are the answers to the bottle names containing champagne:

Magnum	2 bottles
Jeroboam	4 bottles
Rehoboam	6 bottles
Methuselah	8 bottles
Salmanazar	12 bottles
Balthazar	16 bottles
Nebuchadnezzar	20 standard bottles (usually for display).

The Loire

The Loire, the longest river in France, produces a considerable variety of wines of different character, mainly because of the many hundreds of miles, 600 to be precise, that this viticultural area covers, from the Atlantic coast near Nantes, towards the town of Pouilly-sur-Loire just 80 miles from the Côte d'Or, in the east.

Muscadet wines are produced near the mouth of the river. This is a light, dry white wine a favourite for every blackboard; a good choice of wine to accompany fish dishes, including oysters, and other shellfish.

Sancerre made from the Sauvignon grape is a crisp wine and like the wines of Pouilly-sur-Loire has a character often described as 'flinty'.

Pouilly Fumé Be careful not to mix this up with the white *Mâcon* (*Pouilly Fuissé*) of the Burgundy area. Pouilly Fumé produces a fine, long-living dry white wine with a distinctive and attractive bouquet. The wine called *Pouilly-sur-Loire* is best drunk quite cold, and is produced from the less fine Chasselas grape.

Anjou is best known here in England for its slightly sweet rosé, but it also produces some very drinkable white wines, including *Savennières* in the Côteaux de la Loire. Quarts de Chaume and Bonnezeaux, from the Côteaux du Layon produce fine Sauternes-like wines, and are well worth familiarising yourself with.

Saumur like *Vouvray* in Touraine produces some splendid sparkling wines, very popular as a second choice to champagne here in England. It also produces fine white wines varying from dry to sweet.

Touraine, like Anjou, an ancient province has a larger production of red wines than Anjou, some of them really worth trying, especially for anyone looking for an alternative to the ubiquitous Beaujolais. Distinctive in flavour, the red wines to look for here come from Chinon and Bourgueil where like new Beaujolais, the exception to the rule applies when the wine is served stone cold.

Bourqueil and **St Nicholas de Bourqueil** are reputed to be the best of the reds in the Loire.

The Rhône

The long extensive valley of the Rhône stretches from Lyon in the north to Avignon in the south. The northern districts of Condrieu and Hermitage are cut off from the southern area comprising Lirac, Tavel, Rasteau, Beaumes-de-Venise and Châteauneuf du Pape. The reason for this 'gap' 40 kilometres (25 miles) long is because the middle of the valley is without vines. The difference in climate between the two areas is quite marked. In the north the locals enjoy a typical temperate continental climate with warm summers and mild winters. The south is quite Mediterranean with hot, dry summers and cool winters. The whole region is subject to wind, known as the 'Mistral' which is a result of cool air from the Alps flowing downwards into the plains at a rate of some 48 to 64 miles per hour. Not only the vines have to be tough to survive here, so do the people.

Many different grape varieties may be used for the wines of this region, but in the north Syrah is an important grape whilst in the south Grenache predominates. The wines from the south are described as the 'big' wines because of their fullness and strength. As it now seems accepted practice to enjoy a glass of wine with a good meal, the wines of the Rhône valley are becoming increasingly popular here in England and 'good buys' are often to be found from this area. Look out for wines from:

Côtes du Rhône – these will probably have a vineyard or brand name on the label. Soft and full of flavour, these are dark or medium-dark red wines.

Côte Rôtie – a wine made principally from the Syrah grape with about 20 per cent of Viognier added. Sometimes this is described as a cross between a Burgundy and a Claret.

Condrieu – a white wine from the Viognier grape, full bodied and long lasting.

Chateau Grillet – produces a famous, rich white wine at times made from grapes which have been affected by 'Pourriture Noble'. However as production is small, some years less than a thousand bottles, it is quite a rarity, and is the smallest A.C. in France.

St Joseph – red wines from the Syrah grape which are full and fruity, though the area also produces some white wines with Appellation Controlée approval which are worth trying.

Hermitage (or Ermitage) and **Crozes Hermitage** – the famous Hermitage vineyards lie just above the town of Tain-l-Hermitage. The town takes its name from a knight crusader (the Chevalier de Sterimbourg) who when he hung up his sword in exchange for a pair of secateurs decided to

Make wine not war!

make his home in the vineyards. The red full-bodied wines are grown on granite soil from the Syrah grape. *Hermitage* is slow to mature, maybe ten or more years are needed to reveal its deep colour and distinctive bouquet. Bought as a young wine it can prove to be a 'good buy' for any wine lover. The white wines with a full bouquet are dry and delicate. These are made from the Marsanne and Rousanne grapes grown on suitable chalky earth.

Crozes Hermitage – yet another fine wine produced from the vineyards surrounding Hermitage. These slightly cheaper and more easily available wines are lighter but an excellent alternative worthy of a try.

Clairette de Die – an excellent white or sparkling rosé wine produced here from the Clairette grape; a grape grown extensively in Southern France.

Châteauneuf du Pape and **Tavel** – the two most famous names in the Southern part of the Côtes du Rhône.

In 1309 Clement V was crowned as Pope. Pape Clement was the first occupant of a castle in the Rhône, halfway between Avignon and Orange, called Chateauneuf du Pape. The long established vineyard enjoys a fine reputation and produces much full-bodied red wine and less interesting white. Soft and deceptively strong, as many as thirteen grape varieties are commonly used, Grenache, Syrah, Cinsault and others. The reds offer excellent value for money and it is wrongly said that they lack the breeding of Burgundy. They are suitable for early drinking though you will be repaid for keeping them three, four years or more.

Tavel – the other big name is home to a dark, orangy-brown rosé. Unlike most rosé wines, those of Tavel and Lirac are produced from a mixture of red and white grapes, fermented together. Described as onion-skin coloured, *Tavel* has a high alcohol content. It has a more distinctive flavour than the rosés of Anjou and is dryer. When young and relatively cheap these wines drink well, but the fine flavour is considered by some experienced wine-knows to improve in the bottle for up to some ten years.

Beaumes de Venise – one of the best V. D. N. from France, ideal as an aperitif served very cold, or at times as a dessert wine.

Let's not forget the excellence of Red Gigondas and Côtes Ventaux among many more Rhône wines worthy of consideration.

Other Wines of France

The remaining areas of France – the Jura, Languedoc, Roussillon and Provence – are a mixture of V. D. Q. s and table wines, though many have been elevated to Appellation Contrôlée standard. These vary but some bargains are to be found. Provence wines are strong and pink, the most notable from Cassis – not to be confused with 'Crème de Cassis' the blackcurrant liqueur from Dijon great for adding to rather dry acid white wines to produce the sometime fashionable drink called 'Kir'.

Other Appellation Contrôlée districts are A. C. Palette, A. C. Bandol, and A. C. Ballet.

Languedoc and **Roussillon** cover the Mediterranean coast from the Spanish frontier to Italy.

Fitou is enjoying some attention here in England at present, a soft red wine made from the Spanish grape Carignan fermented with a small percentage of white grapes. 'Bag in a box' lovers will no doubt know the names of Côtes du Languedoc, Minervois, Costieres du Gard and Corbières.

Clairette du Languedoc – a full bodied white wine is worth looking out for, as is the Champagne Method-made white wine – Blanquette de Limoux. A small area west of Languedoc producing a large quantity of this sparkling white from the Mauzac grape.

Jura

Rarely seen outside France the wines of the Jura are varied and unusual to say the least, producing red, white, grey, yellow and 'Mad' wines. The latter, from L'Etoile, refers to a sparkling white wine from Arbois. This is the town from which Pasteur wrote his famous treatise on wine.

For the inhabitants of Arbois half the year is spent busy with the vineyards, for the rest of the time, clock- and watch-making keep the locals occupied. The *Vin Jaunes*, or yellow wines, are yellowish-amber coloured, resembling a dry sherry in flavour and bouquet. The speciality of the region,

Time and vine wait for no man!

it is bottled in dumpy bottles called 'clavelins'. Straw wines are made by leaving the grapes on straw mats for two or three months to dry out and these are the rarest wines of France.

Savoie white wines by contrast are totally colourless, soft and gentle, the best coming from Crepy and Seyssel where the vineyards are scattered on mountainous countryside. This area is known for producing some excellent 'sparkling' wines.

Vin-Doux-Naturels This is little known in Britain, a wine in which some of the natural sugar of the grape is prevented from fermenting – by the addition of brandy – in other words, fortified, like port. These are extensively used in the sweetening of vermouths. The Madeira-like taste comes from the casks which, unlike port, are quite often left open to the cold of winter and heat of summer for the wines to mature.

A. C. Banyuls from the Grenache grape is highly thought of. Also with a higher minimum degree of alcohol and usually aged more.

A. C. Banyuls Grand Crû Another Vin-doux-Naturels from the Muscat grape, more costly than the ordinary A. C. Banyuls.

A. C. Muscat de Rivesaltes The flavour of the fine fresh Muscat grapes from which this wine is made predominates.

The contents of the bottle.

The year of harvest.

Michelsberg is the collective name given to the group of vineyards in which the village of Piesport is located.

The larger region from which the wine comes.

Official quality testing number, given only after rigorous examination.

Bottler's name and address.

Refers to category of wine. Here a Qualitätswein.

A typical German wine label

5 *Germany*

Understanding the Label

Germany has new wine laws and quality controls which will assist you with identification, whilst also helping to guarantee standards.

Besides the description, the label may also include the vintage, the vineyard, the grape variety and the name of the 'wine grower'.

If you are able to understand and memorise these categories and descriptions you will, I am sure, find it most helpful in interpreting German wine labels. Such knowledge will add greatly to your enjoyment of a broad range of beautiful wines.

Description of ordinary table wine	Description of table wine from a particular region	Quality wine	Top quality wine
Deutscher Tafelwein	Landwein	Qualitätswein (Qba)	Qualitätswein mit Prädikat (QmP), described in ascending order as Kabinett, Spätlese, Auslese, Beerenauslese or Trockenbeerenauslese and Eiswein

74

German Wine Words

Auslese	Quality wine from selected overripe grapes
Aus eigenem losegut	From producer's own vineyard
Beerenauslese	Wine from grapes hand picked from selected late picked, noble-rot affected grapes
Bereich	Sub-division of a German wine region
Deutscher sekt	German sparkling wine which must have three-fifths German wine in it
Edel	Noble, referring to wine or spirits
Edelfäule	Noble rot or mould in overripe grapes which helps produce magnificent wine
Eigene abfullung	Producer's own bottling
Eiswein	Wine made from frozen grapes - very rare
Grosslage	Sub division of a bereich
Kabinett	Lowest grade of top quality wine - sweet
Most	Must
Pruf (with number) or Prufungsnummer	Testing reference number on label

Qualitätswein	Middle of the three German wine grades
Qualitätswein mit pradikat	Top grade German wine
Roseewein	Rosé from red grapes
Rotling	Rosé from red and white grapes
Schaumwein	Sparkling wine
Sekt	Sparkling wine (German produced)
Spätlese	From late picked grapes
Tafelwein	Ordinary table wine
Trocken	Dry
Trockenbeeren-auslese	Top quality wine made from overripe grapes which are hand picked from selected bunches
Weingarten	Vineyard
Weinkellerie	Wine cellars
Weissherbst	Same as roseewein - but from a specific grape
Weisswein	White wine
Winzergenossen-schaft	Winegrowers' Co-operative
Winzerverein	"

Popular wines	Pronounciations
Auslese	Aws laiser
Beerenauslese	Beeren-aws-laiser
Bernkastle	Bairn-kastel
Gewurztraminer	Gerwerts trameener
Kabinett	Cabin-ette
Mosel/Moselle	Moh-zell
Nahe	Nah
Nierstein	Neer-stine
Piesport	Peas-port
Piesporter	Peas porter
Goldtropchen	Gold-trup-shen
Rheingau	Rine-gowe
Rheinhessen	Rine hessin
Riesling	Reess-ling
Ruwer	Roover
Spätlese	Schpayt-laiser
Stein	Shtine
Steinwein	Shtine-vine

Trocken
Beerenauslese   Trocken-beeren-owslaiser
Worms   Vorms

Although Germany is not one of the large wine-producing countries it is home to some of the world's finest white wines. Its Rhine and Moselle wines are amongst the most notable. Due to the German vineyards lying at the northern limit of successful viticulture, there is a constant struggle with the elements, and German winemakers must therefore take greater care than those in more favourable climes. However, success with wine production has been achieved and improved upon since Roman times.

Most of the vineyards are situated on steep hills on the banks of the river Rhine, running from Worms to Koblenz. The Moselle, a quite different river, runs through green covered hills joining the Rhine at Koblenz. These green covered hills are deceptive as they are composed of slaty rock and back-breaking labour is required to cultivate them.

The principal growing areas are Moselle, Mosel-Saar Ruwer, Rheinhessen, and Rheingau, Nahe, Franconia and Rheinpfalz. The provinces of Württemburg and Baden nearer to the Swiss border also produce good wines, although they are not exported in any great quantity.

Whilst German winemakers do not resort to short cuts, most of Germany's quality control system is tied up to modern science and technology. As I have explained, the German climate is somewhat

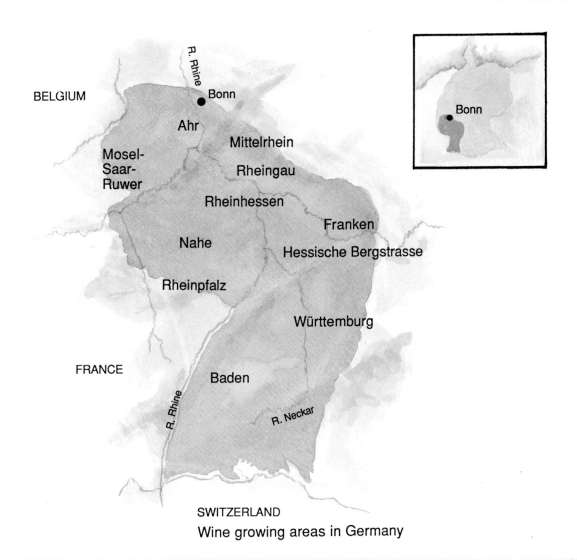

BELGIUM

R. Rhine

Bonn

Ahr

Mittelrhein

Mosel-
Saar-
Ruwer

Rheingau

Rheinhessen

Franken

Nahe

Hessische Bergstrasse

Rheinpfalz

Württemburg

FRANCE

Baden

R. Rhine

R. Neckar

SWITZERLAND

Wine growing areas in Germany

Bonn

unpredictable, and the prolonged autumn weather needed for the grapes to ripen to their sweetest does not always occur. In a bad year entirely natural wines will not be sweet, in fact, they can be quite undrinkable. Therefore, it is a standard and necessary practice to *sweeten* the wines by the addition of sugar. This is in order to obtain the correct balance of sweetness and acidity. The modern method is to add sweetening in the form of unfermented grape juice towards the end of the natural fermentation. A very fine filter process removes the yeasts thus preventing the grape juice from fermenting. This practice of adding the grape juice of 'Süss-Reserve' is sometimes criticised, but German growers are concerned only with producing the best wines and this blending and sweetening operation is necessary in order to produce 'Qualitätswein' or 'Pradikatswein', wine with a satisfactory balance of sugar and alcohol, according to very strict rules and regulations.

The Moselle or Mosel

Main grapes - Riesling, Ebling, Müller-Thurgau.

A twisting meandering river, dotted with picture-book towns and villages, the area is densely planted with vines. The Moselle's powerfully scented wines have a touch of acidity derived from the grey slate soil. Nevertheless, the wines provide gentle, easy drinking, best drunk young when they are crisp and fresh. Correctly chilled they make excellent wines for a party. Sometimes referred to as 'German Shlurpers' as they are unlikely to tire the

I'll be glad when I've had enough!

system even when drunk in large quantities.

Names such as Piesport and Bernkastle will no doubt be familiar to you. The best vineyards in the Mittel Moselle quite often have pictures of the area on the label as the scenery is so impressive. The Saar and the Ruwer, two important contributaries join the Moselle from the east. These tributaries and the land between them make up the Beriech Saar Ruwer. Sometimes if the summer weather is not favourable, they are almost unable to produce anything of consequence, in fact, a wine known as 'Dreimannerwein' or three-man wine, is produced. It simply means it takes two men to hold down the third man to make him drink it!

Franconia (Franken)

Vineyards are scattered all over this region in the hope of catching the best of the sun and the soil. Lying on both sides of the river Main, it is the most easterly of all the Germany QbA regions. The old cathedral city of Würzburg is home to the principal wine of the region – *Würzburger Stein*. *Steinwein* is the name generally given to the Franconian wines although strictly speaking German law reserves the name for this vineyard only. It is traditionally sold in a flat flagon-shaped bottle called a Bocksbeutel. Because the soil of the area varies considerably, type and quality is variable. The wines have a flavour all of their own – on the whole they are dry and flinty, but do have a tendency to become rather acidy due to the cold winters and late springs.

Worth getting into hock for!

Rheingau

An area much visited by Queen Victoria, it is situated on the foothills of the Taunus mountains. Fuller and longer lasting wines come from the Rhine, some of the finest from Johannisberg, Rudesheim, Rauenthal, Hallgarten, Erbach and Hocheim. Hocheim is the wine Queen Victoria would request if she fancied a tipple – 'Bring me a glass of Mein Hock' and so the name hock has been in the English language ever since.

Nahe and Rheinhessen

As hock enthusiasts will know, hocks come from four well defined areas. Besides Rheingau there is the Nahe, the river joining the Rhine near Bingen. It produces practically no red wines but the crisp fruity whites are similar to wines of the Rheingau. On the opposite side of the Rhine in Rheinhessen most of the wine grown is the sweetish *Liebfraumilch*, the name taken from the Liebfrauenkirche (church) in the city of Worms, which has its own vineyard. The name became so popular that others have used it, although it is now controlled and may only come from Rheinhessen, Nahe and Rheinpfalz.

Rheinpfalz

Based on the slopes of the rain-protecting Haardt mountains the area enjoys a warmer and sunnier climate than most other parts of Germany. Warm enough in fact to grow things like lemons, figs and almonds, vineyard names such as Mandelgarten (almond grove) are to be found. The region produces more red than Rheingau or Rheinhessen, from the Portugieser grape. A variety of grapes are grown for the white wines of which many are sweetish and rather heady – the sweetest coming from Forst, which at its best is sometimes comparable with the great Sauternes of France for its richness and flavour.

German Sparklers

Known as Sekt, sparkling wines are produced all over Germany. The best qualities come from the Moselle and good Rhine vineyards – mostly in the Mittel-Rhein. Single vineyard sparkling wines are made at Steinberg, and Johannisberg. From Württemberg you have a sparkling wine which is red. Sometimes Sekt is made as in the champagne area, but most is made by the tank method or cuvé closé.

6 *Italy*

Understanding the Label

Although in 1963 the government tightened regulations to improve standards, correct and modernise cultivation methods, the labelling and categories of the wines still remains a little confusing. Italian wines may be given their names according to a grape, a district, a 'style' of wine or even some romantic 'nickname'. The D.O.C. laws have at least ensured regional information is on the labels of the classified wines. The knowledge of wine words will be most helpful to you here.

Description of ordinary table wine	Description of table wine from a particular region	Quality wine	Top quality wine
Vino da tavola	Denominazione d'Origine Simplici (DOS)	Denominazione d' Origine Controllata (DOC)	Denominazione d' Origine Controllata e Garantia (DOCG)

The Vintage Year.

Brand name – not a wine name.

Soave is a region in Northern Italy. East of Verona, producing fresh white wine of attractive texture.

Name and address of bottler in Italy.

D.O.C. the control governing the true origin of the wine.

The contents of the bottle in centilitres. The e denotes that the contents comply with E.E.C regulations.

A typical Italian wine label

Italian Wine Words

Abboccato	Sweet
Amabile	Sweetish
Annata	Year - vintage
Amaro	Very dry or bitter
Azienda	Estate Farm
Beva Fresca	Fresh wine
Bianco	White
Cantina	Winery
Casa Vinicola	Wine Company
Chiaretto	Light red
Classico	From the best central vineyards of a region
Colli	Hills
Consorzio	Winegrowers' Association
Dolce	Very sweet
Fattoria	Farm Estate
Fiasco	Flask such as chianti bottle
Frizzante	Wine that is slightly sparkling

Gradi alcool	Alcohol strength
Imbottigliato QA	Bottled by
Nero	Dark red colour (of wine)
Riserva	Better quality wine - aged in wood and bottle
Rosato	Pink (Rosé)
Rosso	Red
Secco	Dry
Spumante	Sparkling
Superiore	Wine meeting higher DOC standards
Tenuta	Estate
Vecchio	Old
Vino da Pasto	Ordinary wine
Vino Novello	New wine

Popular Wines   Pronounciations

Asti Spumante	Ass-tea-spoomantay
Chianti	Key-ann-tea
Valpolicella	Val-pol-ee chelah
Verdicchio	Var-deeckyoh

The old adage, quantity rather than quality, is sometimes applied to the wines of Italy, for Italy produces more wine than any other country, almost *every year.*

The cheap and cheerful image that Italian wines have here in England is perhaps a little deceptive as some of Italy's best producers have been making reliable wines for a long time. The quality is steadily improving under present laws, and Italian wines can now provide good value for money and, from time to time, exceptional wines.

Northern Italy

Piemont (Piemonte) – This area is responsible for the production of Asti Spumante, a light golden wine with a sweet and delicate taste, resulting from the Muscat or Muscato grape from which it is made. The town of Asti is right in the centre of this region. The area produces both still and sparkling wines, the Spumante being the sparkling version and is mostly made in 'tanks', however, a proportion is made by the traditional method, like champagne, but it has little in common with champagne.

Also from this area come Italy's fine red wines, *Barolo* and *Barbaresco*. Barolo a 'big' fruity, dark, powerful wine with long lasting characteristics. It is made from the Nebbiolo grape and has an unmistakable flavour and scent. A little less expensive, though very similar, Barbaresco is from further down the mountainside and is a wine which is less mouthfilling and just a wee bit drier. Both these wines have been given D.O.C.G. status.

The other red wines of Piemont are called by the grapes from which they are produced, probably the best known being *Grignolino*, *Nebbiolo* and *Barbaresco*. A great deal of Piemont wine goes into the production of vermouth in Turin.

North-East Italy

Verona on the other side of Lake Garda, is the centre of this wine producing area. The famous *Valpolicella, Soave* and *Bardolino* all come from these hills. Valpolicella which should be drunk young is light and pale and quite a contrast to Barolo and Barbaresco, as is Bardolino which is so pale it could almost be a rosé. Easy drinking is Italy's *Soave*, best before it reaches three years old. Considered to be Italy's best white wine, straightforward, a little unthrilling, it is light and dry and is reasonable value for money.

The Italian Tyrol, to the north of Verona, is Italy's most northern region and produces *Trentino* and *Alto Adige*. In fact German is spoken as much as Italian. The range of red and white wines are similar in character to those of Germany and Austria and the labels will often be found in either language.

The best red wine of the area – *Santa Maddelena* or – in German – St

Magdalener stand up well to other Italian red wines, deep in colour with good body it makes pleasant drinking; although not easily available outside Italy.

Lago di Caldaro, also called Kalteresee is, however, to be found in reasonable quantities. Here near the Tyrol the grapes such as Traminer, which originated in this region, and Riesling, give their names to the white wines which are Germanic in character.

Central Italy

Lambrusco, sweet red and sparkling, comes from a group of ten communes of the county of Emilia-Romana. Its name comes from the grape and is popular for pleasant drinking outside of Italy.

Chianti from the hills between Florence and Sienna in Tuscany is Italy's best known wine. The fast disappearing straw-covered bottle is being replaced by claret-shaped bottles. It is said that no wine other than Beaujolais has ever been faked more than Chianti; its producers have had great difficulty protecting its famous name. Genuine Chianti comes from certain specified areas, the central and oldest category is Chianti Classico which has D.O.C. status. Look for a black cockerel on a gold background on the label at the neck of the bottle, as the authentic sign of a group of Chianti makers who believe in standards and continuity. The other Chiantis

Wine growing areas of Italy

have place or district names – *Chianti Rufina* being amongst the best. Chiantis allowed to age for two years maybe described as Vecchio (old), provided it has a minimum of 12° alcohol content, (12.5° for classico). Those matured for at least five years may be called Riserva – in a different class to other Chiantis it is one of Italy's finest wines.

Brunello di Montalcino – as the name implies, is made from the Brunello grape in the village of Montalcino, south of Sienna. One of the best red wines of Italy it is a full-bodied, well-balanced wine but because it is regarded as exceptional and is scarce, it does command very high prices. It now has D.O.C.G. status as well as the Vino Nobile di Montepulciano.

Umbria – is still further south right in the centre of Italy and produces renowned wines. The old Etruscan town of Orvieto gives the wine its name. Made from 4 grapes including the Trevviano grape this famous white wine can be sweet – *Orvieto Abbocato* – made from rotting grapes (Muffa Nobile – see page 53) or refreshingly dry *Orvieto Secco* which matures in cellars cut out of rock beneath the city itself. Red Orvieto is also very well thought of.

Lazio. These Roman wines are white, a pleasant wine called *Frascati* is the best known. It is in this part of the country – in the village of Montefiascone that one of the wine's historic stories comes. A wine called *Est! Est! Est!* is so called because a German Bishop, named Fugger, was travelling to Rome for the coronation of Emperor Henry V. As he didn't have the benefit of a *Guide Michelin* he sent his manservant ahead to arrange rooms at suitable inns, and to mark those with especially good wine. In order to do this the servant wrote the word 'Est' upon the door, this being an abbreviation for the Latin 'Vinum Bonum Est' – the wine is good. On reaching the inn at Montefiascone the wine was apparently so good that he was elated and awarded three accolades, he wrote on the door – Est! Est! Est! (It is, It is, It is). In fact the inn was so good too that the Bishop hung up his mitre and cloak here and remained in Montefiascone until the end of his days where it is said he is buried in the local churchyard.

Verdicchio de Castelli di Jesi is a D.O.C. area on the east coast, lying inland from Ancona near the town of Jesi. A very pleasant dry crisp wine, it is sold in vase shaped green bottles and is well known to all tourists.

Southern Italy

Lacrima Christi produced on the seaward slopes of Vesuvius is a good white sweet wine much imitated under various spellings. One must look for the names of reliable growers to be sure of good wine. Red and rosé wine is also produced.

Ravello, red and white is one of the South's better wines.

'The service here isn't what it used to be!'

Marsala is the Italian equivalent of sherry, though quite uncomparable in flavour, and is the best known wine from Sicily. Drunk as an aperitif it is a rich fortified wine which may be either dry or sweet.

Wine growing areas in Spain and Portugal

7 *The Iberian Peninsula*

Sherry and Port spring to mind when one thinks of Spain and Portugal. However, these are fortified wines which I shall explain later.

Both these countries produce excellent light wines, which are available here in England.

Some Spanish wines here have adopted the rather derogatory title of 'plonk'. It is said this term is derived from the English Soldiers' (1914) inability to pronounce 'blanc' (white), not a problem for wine-knows now!

Wine words

Spain

Anos	Years
Blanco	White wine
Clarete	Light, red or dark rosé
Consejo regulador	Wine Control Association
Corsecho	Crop – Vintage

Denomination de origen	Wine control status
Dulce	Sweet
Embotellado de origen	Estate bottled
Engarrando de origen	Estate bottled
Espumoso	Sparkling
Fino	Very dry and very pale sherry
Flor	Film which appears on a very dry sherry
Reserva	Mature wine
Tinto	Red wine
Vendimia	Vintage
Vina	Vineyard

Portugal

Adamo	Sweet
Adega	Wine cellar
Branco	White wine
Clarete	Light red or dark rosé

Denominacao do Origem	Wine Control Status
Espumante	Sparkling
Garrafeira	Best quality
Regaio Demarcada	Legally defined area
Seco	Dry
Vinha	Vineyard
Vino da consumo	Ordinary wine
Vino de mesa	Table wine
*Vinho verde**	Young wine

*(Vinho verde is pronounced veenyoosh vaideh)

Whilst Spain does produce plenty of 'plonk' it also produces some better quality wines from favoured areas. The generally most controlled wines are from *Rioja, Tarragona, Valencia, Alicante* and *Malaga*.

Rioja – A region on the upper reaches of the Ebro river, produces both red and white. From the Tempranillo and Garnach grapes come the deep ruby-red tintos which are delicious and full bodied.

The claretes are at times lighter with a marked bouquet and character. The white wines (blancos) are best when dry, the colour varying between green and gold in colour. Rosé wines of different strengths and dryness are also exported from this region.

Tarragona produces a large proportion of red and white table wines, shipped to Britain under brand names and described simply as Spanish red or white wines.

Penedes noted for dry white wines which are excellent for serving with shellfish. This area also produces a large amount of sparkling wines, or espumosos. Some of these sparkling wines are produced by a second fermentation in the bottle as in champagne and some by the 'tank' or impregnation method. Labelled according to their sweetness Spanish 'sparklers' range from:

Bruto – extra dry
Seco – dry
Semiseco – semi dry
Semidulce – semi sweet
Dulce – sweet

Portugal

Portugal is quite a contrast to Spain in geography and climate. As opposed to the plains of Spain, Portugal produces a wetter climate in all but the summer months reflecting a difference of the wines.

This is the land of the *Vinhos Verdes* or greenwines; this is not a description of the colour of the wine, but are so called because they are made from underipe or 'green' grapes. The region lies between the river Minho and the river Dauro. Here the grapes are grown on high trellises about 8 feet off the ground. This provides cover for food crops below, although the grapes are denied reflected heat from the soil. The foliage provides protection for the grapes from direct sun rays. These less sweet grapes contain more malic acid resulting in the production of wines with a slight sparkle or 'petillants', due to small degrees of fermentation in the bottles. Grilled sardines and *Vinho Verde* served by the quayside is wonderful if you enjoy good digestion!

Bucelas and **Dao** are names to look for and produce maduro or mature wines, which have spent an average of two years in the barrel.

Colares – made from ungrafted vines, is a long lasting red wine, and though not like claret maintains some of its qualities.

Fortified Wines

Sherry

Sherry 'styles' are made in several places, Cyprus and Australia. British sherry, widely advertised at Christmas, is made from grape concentrate imported from abroad. True sherry comes only from southern Spain in the

A tall order

Jerez (pronounced Hereth) region. The wine there is made by a special, traditional process.

Pale and dry is Fino
Medium is Amontillado
Dark and Sweet is Oloroso
Cream is always sweet and may be either dark or pale.

Port

Again, port-style dessert wines are made other than in the northern parts of Portugal, which is the Douro region where port comes from. I occasionally enjoy a dry white port (which is made from white grapes) as an aperitif but red and sweet is the traditional port.

The youngest port is ruby
A more mature blend of ruby is tawny
The top of the range is Vintage and is made from the wine of a single year which after two years in a cask is bottled and matured with careful keeping in the bottle
Late bottled Vintage is kept in a cask for five years and then bottled, it leaves no sediment and is less expensive than vintage
Crusted port is made from a blend of different vintages

⑧ *Other Wines of the World*

Switzerland

Since time immemorial vines have been grown on the steep hillsides and mountain terraces on the northern shore of Lake Geneva. Now mainly the Chasselas grape variety, known locally as the Fendant, is favourite for the white wines produced here. From the Pinot and Gamay grape Switzerland does produce some red wines. Whilst it is always interesting to try different wines from different countries, it is perhaps fair to say that preferable alternatives for the 'types ' of wine made in Switzerland can be found.

Austria

No doubt having some difficulty living down the 'Anti-Freeze' scandal of 1986, Austria's best wines are white (mainly German style) although red is also produced. *Schluck*, a name you may recognise, is a rather sweet wine from a beautiful area on the River Danube. Tischweine is the name for Austrian table wine, for a better quality look for the word 'Spitzenweine'.

Hungary

From the town of Eger comes 'Bulls Blood' now only available in 'Estate Bottled' from a specific area. Not only can the name be off-putting but when drunk rather young it can seem rough. However, when left to age a little this red wine made from the Kekfrankos and Kadarka grapes can develop into a fine full-bodied wine.

Hungary is also known for the fabled sweet *Tokay Aszu*, a wine made from grapes which have been affected by the 'Noble Rot', (see page 00) called Aszu berries. These berries are crushed by their own weight in tubs called Puttonyi, then they are pounded to a paste. The paste is then added to the normal wine must to determine the final quality and sweetness of the resulting *Tokay Aszu*. Dry Tokay wines are also produced from grapes from which the Aszu grapes have not been separated, these will be labelled *Tokay Szamorodni*.

Yugoslavia

As Yugoslavia has been more successful in introducing her wines to Britain than other Eastern European countries, you may well be familiar with the wine *Lutomer Riesling*. A refreshing medium wine with a delicate bouquet it is made from the Laski Riesling grape, an Italian cousin of the true German Riesling. A little sweeter and rounder is the *Lutomer Sylvaner*.

Whilst popular with connoisseurs because of its delicate bouquet, and slightly more pronounced taste, the *Lutomer Traminer* is worth looking out for. The rather rich *Ranina Radgona* or 'Tiger's Milk' made from selected late picked frapes has similar qualities of a *Spätlese* wine and comes from the north-east of the country.

Less successful are the Yugoslavian red wines.

Bulgaria

Bulgaria where the wines are generally named after the grapes, has more recently proved to be successful in the wine industry. Exports are encouraged, *Cabernet Sauvignon* from the Sakar Mountains and the *Merlot* from *Trakia* are reasonable value single grape variety wines you may come across. The Sauvignons and Chardonnays are the more appealing of the white wines produced in Bulgaria.

Cyprus

This is one of the oldest wine producing areas in the world. *Commandaria*, a powerful syrupy dessert wine, is named after the wine that was made from grapes grown in the Commandaria of the Knights Templars! Nowadays you will find Cyprus wines here in Britain. Good red wines such as *Othello* and of course a great deal of sherry consumed here comes from Cyprus.

Greece

Again this country has a long history of wine making. Possibly most famous for here resinated wines (wines to which strongly scented resins have been added) these are perhaps an acquired taste which some find enjoyable. *Pallini* – a semi-sweet white wine, and *Mavrodaphne* are amongst the unresinated wines produced, with a high alcohol content.

Australia

Few people would associate Australia with wine production, but it is a fact that wine has been produced here for almost two centuries. A Captain John McArthur was responsible for developing Australia's wine production on a commercial scale. Despite a shaky start, having his brandy stills confiscated and being tried in the criminal courts for attempting to produce spirit illegally, McArthur went on to develop his winery with the aid of his two sons.

The Australian wine industry has a strong link with European traditions, most of the vines come from the finest vineyards of France and Germany. Therefore it is hardly surprising that coupled with an abundance of sunshine to ripen the grapes, Australia is able to produce such good wines.

The principle regions are Riverland, South Australia, Murrumbidgee Irrigation Area in New South Wales, North East Victoria, the Barossa and Hunter Valleys and the Clare, South Australia.

'No flies on me when it comes to wine, cobber"

A lively range of red and white wines are produced. Noble grape varieties Cabernet Sauvignon, Merlot, Malbec, Pinot Noir, Shiraz and others are used. The Shiraz blended with Cabernet Sauvignon produces an outstanding dry red wine, full and fruity with good balance. The Riesling grape is used in the production of a good white wine. Although supplies of Australian wines are filtering through to Britain, it could not really be described as widely available. But this situation is rapidly changing, and Australian Chardonnay is a white wine well worth looking for.

New Zealand

Only recently, in the last 20 years or so, has New Zealand been making wine on a commercial basis. A trip to the local supermarket will reveal they are available. Mainly from German grape varieties like Müller-Thurgan, you may see also Cooks Wines, Cabernet Sauvignon, Gewurtztraminer and Chardonnay, all representing good value.

Turkey, Syria, Lebanon, Israel, Egypt, Malta, The Soviet Union, and Czechoslovakia

These all produce wine of varying qualities.

North-West Africa, Tunisia, Algeria and Morocco

These also cultivate the vine, though the local Moslem religion forbids drinking of alcohol.

The Americas (Chile, Brazil , Argentina)

There are wines produced in these areas which are increasingly seen on our shelves.

North America

Genus Euvitis from which all wine producing vines spring, has existed in North America as long as man. Wine is made in several states.

California

This is by far the largest producer. In the last 130 years Californian wines have come to be taken seriously. California consists of a series of ranges and valleys, running NNE to SSW, between the Pacific Ocean and the Rocky mountains. The winters are cold especially in Oregon to the North. The summers are Mediterranean and the vineyards have to be irrigated by

'I'm only here to surf you!'

spraying. Vineyards and other fruit crops take priority for water during the hot weather.

The Napa Valley produces some exceptional red wines from the grape of the area. Cabernet Sauvignon is often thought to be on a par with some of the fine clarets of Bordeaux. The price can sometimes reflect this, Zifandel, California's own grape variety, is a name you may come across, possibly produced from the wineries of Paul Masson or Almadern. The Salinas Valley, the Samona Valley to the North of San Francisco, and Monterey County to the South, also produce wines of various 'styles'. Riesling and Chardonnay wines can be truly outstanding and an excellent 'champagne' is to be found. Reduced to simple terms, given time, the wines of California are a good contender for quality wine production, level with many of the wines of Europe.

Also from California (and other vineyards of the world) come the 'Blush' wines. After crushing, the juice is allowed a brief period of skin contact prior to pressing, and a long, cool fermentation. Producing delicate, light wines with a pale salmon hue, these wines are clear, fruity and fresh. Moderately chilled they would make an ideal aperitif, or wine to drink with light food.

England

An expanding range of reputable wines, grown against the climatic odds.

Part Three

The Practical Things

'May I suggest you read *How To Be A Wine-Know?*'

9 **Buying**

Though there are not many wine merchants available to assist you at the supermarket 'cellar' you do in many supermarkets have the advantage of a grading system. For example, numbers 1-3 are medium-dry wines, or 5-6 rather sweeter. (Full details of the scale are given on the following pages.) However, what do you do when you enter the wine merchants who don't provide this information? The obvious choice is to march right up to the counter and explain:

- The occasion
- The amount you wish to spend
- The type of food you wish to serve with it
- Most important of all, the kind of wine you as host most enjoy drinking.

Don't feel inhibited by his knowledge, you know when you enter the shop/warehouse roughly what you are looking for and most wine merchants will be happy to assist. After all he is there to sell and in order for you to visit him again he will advise you to the best of his ability. As you are fast becoming a wine-know you will understand by now the type of wine available to you and can interpret the labels you are looking at. Does it have,

117

for example, in the case of France 'Appellation Contrôlée' approval or is it a Vin de Pays (table wine from a particular region), or a V.D.Q.S. rating (a grade just below Appellation Contrôlée – Vin Delimité de Qualité Supérieure)?

Most of the same rules apply when ordering in a restaurant;

- Cost
- What you have selected to eat
- Your own palate, white, red, dry, sweet and so on.

You do not have the advantage of a label to interpret here, so seek advice. I know we have all experienced the condescending waiter from time to time, but don't feel intimidated even the most decorated somelier (wine waiter) won't make you feel inferior if he does his job well, and you can gain maximum enjoyment of his cellar. His guidance can be invaluable to you when in doubt. Of course, your memory has to help you when selecting and only with experience will you build of a 'file' of wines you know and enjoy.

This scale of sweetness of White Wines, using numbers 1 to 9 has been drawn up by the Wine Development Board. It is a single unified guide, which I'm sure you will find helpful in your selection. Also, the Wine Development Board have produced a Red Taste Guide to help you identify styles of red wine in terms of total taste, in other words 'the impression on the palate'.

White Wine Guide

Have you ever wondered whether you would enjoy a white wine you haven't tasted before? Have you ever bought a white wine new to you and found it too sweet? (Of course wine has more characteristics than mere dryness or sweetness, but many find their enjoyment of a particular wine is largely dependent on this aspect.)

Though the world of wine is very complex, the Guide is simple. Some wines are available in varying degrees of sweetness, therefore this is not a definite scale, it is a helpful means of identifying wines which are your particular taste. The major white wines of the world, as well as rosés, sherries and vermouths are included, it is simply a matter of finding your preferred number or range of numbers. It is fun and beneficial to your expanding knowledge to try wines from different categories.

Bergerac, Muscadet, Touraine, Saumur, Chablis, Entre-Deux-Mers, Pouilly Blanc Fumé, Champagne, Sancerre, Manzanilla Sherry, Tavel Rosé

Graves, Riesling d'Alsace, Frascati Secco, Orvieto Secco, Verdicchio, Soave, Chardonnays, Dry Vouvray, Dry English, Trocken German Wines, White Rioja, White Burgundy, White Rhône, Spanish Dry White, Penedes, Fino Sherry, Dry Sherry Types, Dry Montilla, Sercial Madeira

Pinot Blanc d'Alsace, Brut Sparkling Wine, Muscat d'Alsace, Halb-Trocken German Wines, Hungarian Olasz, Riesling Dry, Gruner Veltliner Austria, Gewurztraminer d'Alsace, Dry Amontillado Sherry, Medium Dry Montilla, Medium Dry Vermouth, Dry White Vermouth, Dry White Port, Medium Dry English

Vinho Verde, Chenin Blancs, Other Gewurztraminers, Rhine QbA, EEC Wines, Mosel Deutscher Tafelwein, Mosel QbA, Rhine and Nahe Kabinett, Yugoslav Laski, and Hungarian Olasz Riesling Medium Dry, Australian, New Zealand and Bulgarian Rieslings, Full Amontillados, Medium Dry Sherry types, Portuguese Rosé, Orvieto Abbocato, Medium English

Rhine Deutscher Tafelwein, Moselle, Spätlesen, Vouvray Demi-Sec, Austrian Spätlesen, Liebfraumilch, Rhine Spätlesen, Medium British Sherry, Verdelho Madeira, Medium White Port

Demi-Sec Sparkling and Demi-Sec Champagne, Tokay Szamarodni Sweet, Spanish Medium, All Golden Sherry types

Asti Spumante, Moselle Auslesen, Rhine Auslesen, Tokay Aszu, Côtes de Bordeaux, Monbazillac, Pale Cream Sherry Montilla Cream, Bual Madeira Rosso, Rosé and Bianco Vermouths

Moselle Beerenauslesen, Austrian Beerenauslesen, Spanish Sweet White, Moscatels, Sauternes, Barsac, Dark Cream Sherry, Cream and Rich Sherry types

Rhine and Austrian Trockenbeerenauslesen, Eiswein, Malmsey Madeira, Muscat de Beaumes de Venise, Marsala, Brown Sherry, Moscatels

Now you can identify, by numbers, all the wines likely to give us most pleasure without the likelihood of disappointment.

Red Wine Taste Guide – The Wine Development Board

As in the case of the successful Dry to Sweet White Wine Guide, the aim is to assist the new or inexperienced red wine drinkers who can be put off by the 'dryness' of red wines. Due to different wine making techniques, and the multiplicity of red wines, the Guide is not a definitive scale.

It is a five point scale, using the letters 'A' to 'E', in order to differentiate it from the White Wine Guide.

The five categories identify red wines in terms of total taste, in other words the 'impression on the palate'.

Starting with 'A', comparable to Beaujolais, the wines are easy, undemanding and quaffable. At 'E' the other end, the wines are bigger and more concentrated 'styles' with a greater sensation of depth and fullness. Italian Barolo, for example, is, generally speaking, more suitable for drinking with food than on its own. It is not intended that fine vintage wines, in other words those destined to mature further in the bottle, should be included in this Guide.

The Guide will help you discover the wines of your choice according to your preference, for the amount of flavour in the wine.

Bardolino, Beaujolais, Valdepenas, EEC Table Wines
German, Red Wines, Touraine, Valdepenas

Côtes du Roussillon, Merlot, Navarra, Red Burgundy,
Pinot Noir from all countries, Valencia, Valpolicella,
Beaujolais Village and Crus, Chinon, Saumur,

Bordeaux Rouge/Claret, Côtes du Rhône, Rioja, Bergerac,
Corbières Minervois

Cabernet Sauvignon from Australia, Bulgaria, California,
Chile, New Zealand, Romania, Dáo, Chateauneuf du Pape,
Chianti Classico, Hungarian Red, Fitou, Médoc

Barolo, Crozes-Hermitage, Cyprus Red, Greek Red and
Shiraz from Australia

What a cork-up!

10 *Handling And Serving*

Good Screws

New streamline versions of the ordinary corkscrew are invented every year! There is little to choose between them all in efficiency – those with counterscrews and levers require less effort. However, the 'screwpull' invented by a Texan is my idea of effortless corkage, ideal for the single girl wanting to impress a male dinner guest: you only need slight pressure to lift the cork and you can save all your energies for later.

Occasionally when opening a bottle, small particles of cork fall into the wine. These can be removed from the glass without any harm to the wine. Correctly, a teaspoon will do the job, but provided they are clean, and don't smell of soap, aftershave or perfume, the tip of one's little finger is the quickest route. Any crystallised sediment in the wine is also harmless.

Opening a Bottle of 'Fizzy'

We've all seen the racing driver drench the entire 'team' with 'fizzy' after winning a race. Festive it may be, but not only is it wasteful it's also messy.

Now, without wishing to be a kill-joy, there is a way to open sparkling wines without losing a third of the bottle's contents.

Hold the bottle at an angle of about 45°, remove the wire and the foil from the cork, keeping a thumb over the cork for safety. Then, holding the cork firmly in one hand, and the bottle in the other, gently twist the *bottle* until the cork eases out, slowly releasing under pressure. This way, no wine should be spilt, providing the wine is well chilled and no one has shaken it beforehand.

Handling and Serving

It adds to the sense of the occasion to treat wine with respect. Moreover, the wine itself actually benefits. In turn, you, the drinker, will gain if you are to get your 'moneysworth', so here are a few basic rules to help you.

Wine in the bottle is still 'alive' and responds to outside conditions so it is important to get these right.

Temperature

Centuries ago it was discovered that white and rosé wines were at their freshest when drunk straight from the cellar (i.e. cold) while most reds needed to warm up to the temperature of the room to develop their full flavour (16–20°C). Few of us have cellars anymore but the rules still hold good.

Red Wines

Room temperature or chambré is exactly what it says, *not* warmed near to a stove or radiator, let alone left standing, as I have seen, 'cooking' in a bowl of hot water!! Most red wines are at their best when they have been exposed to the air. Therefore, if possible, either open the bottle an hour before you need it, or pour the contents into another container, such as a decanter or carafe. Here is a tip for you given to me by a highly thought-of wine man: if you stand your decanter or carafe in a bowl of hot water for a few minutes until it is 'hand warm', and then pour in the chosen wine you will obtain maximum benefit from this quick method to 'chambré' your wine. Be sure not to let any water get into your container as you will not wish to water down the contents! It goes without saying that when 'decanting' a wine containing sediment, this process should be done slowly and carefully with the light behind it so you can see what you are leaving behind in the bottle. You can always put it in the stew!

Incidentally, if you do have a wine containing sediment, leave the bottle standing until it has settled before you decant, or if you've been given one of those wine baskets, this is the time you can actually use it by leaving the wine to settle in it, although this makes opening a little more difficult.

Now, I really don't mean to confuse you but there is an exception to this 'room temperature' rule on the reds. This is for the very light red wines such as young Beaujolais or Valpolicella, which may, if you like, be chilled.

White, Rosé and Sparkling

These all need to be chilled. One or two hours in the fridge is generally enough, over chilling will affect the bouquet and taste. If you are in a hurry an ice bucket with water and ice will do the job. I use an old tall Government Surplus flour bin and three or four of those picnic packs which I always leave in the freezer and it works well. The sweeter the wine the more chilling required – range 4–11°C. You could always stick the bottle in the freezer compartment for ten minutes, but if you have a memory like mine you run the risk of a burst cork or worse, and in any event, extreme cold hides all the flavour and the scent, sorry – bouquet.

11 *Glasses for Wine*

In the same way that attractively served food stimulates the glands of the digestive system, so the more attractively wine is served the more enjoyable it becomes.

The most suitable glasses to choose for wine are the simplest. The classic shape – essentially a bowl on a stem – was specially designed for the wine to be enjoyed to the full.

- It is clear, to show the colour without distortion
- It is narrower at the lip than in the bowl, to concentrate the scent and aroma of the wine, known as the bouquet
- It is generous in size. No wine glass should be more than two-thirds filled, so that there is room in the glass for the bouquet as well as the wine
- It has a stem so that the temperature of your hand need not affect the temperature of the wine

All sorts of different wine glasses are available; some designs follow local traditions in various wine making areas, others merely the whims of the designer. There is absolutely no need to own a full range. You can either

1   2   3   4

use one basic shape as an 'all rounder' for any wine, or for further refinement, slightly different shapes and sizes for different styles of wine.

1. The 'all rounder'. A good sized 'tulip' shaped glass of clear glass is fine for red, white and rosé or sparkling. Indeed, it is much better than the wide 'saucer' glass for sparkling wine which exhausts the bubbles with its large surface area and is very easy to spill. The flute is really best for champagne.

2. Fortified wine, being stronger than table wine, is served in smaller flasses, again with a narrower rim than bowl. If you like to drink sherry 'on the rocks' you will need to use a larger wine glass to make room for the ice.

3. Glasses specially for white wine are generally slimmer and more elegant than those for red.

4. Red wine glasses have a generous bowl, which can easily be cupped in the hand to warm the wine slightly and so release all the aromas. If you do not want to affect the temperature, this too, can be held by the stem.

How much not including aperitifs.

Glass sizes do naturally vary, but as a general rule allow 6–8 glasses per bottle when calculating for entertaining. Allow approximately 3–4 glasses per head to be served with the meal. Although if it is a special occasion and people are relaxing, chatting and enjoying good food, it would be more realistic to make provision for 6–8 glasses per head. Just make sure you have the number of the local taxis handy.

1   2   3   4   5   6

12 *Shapely Bottles*

Many of the wine regions of the world have adopted special shapes of bottles for their products. Some of these may not be used for other wines under government regulations and this indicates to some extent the authenticity of their contents. Look also for 75cl contents, another sign that no price cutting deals have been resorted to.

These are some of the best known *traditional* bottle shapes and sizes used in France and Germany – in those areas you can use this as a guide to their contents, e.g. *Claret* or *Burgundy*. But do watch out, because nowadays other countries do imitate these traditional bottle shapes.

1. Burgundy Bottle – both white and red use similar shape

2. Bordeaux (claret) with well-defined shoulders

3. A Mosel Bottle – Tall, slim and green

4. A Hock or Rhine Bottle – the glass will be brown

5. Needs no explanation – standard **Champagne bottle** 'dressed' and ready for a party

6. An extra: a typical **Port bottle**, good for laying down

13 Keeping and Storing

Here are some hints for keeping and storing wine as *laid down* by the Wine Development Board.

In the days when a lot of houses had cellars, wine was sold before it reached maturity and had to be stored. Now most wine on sale in supermarkets and high street off-licences is ready to drink. But you do not necessarily have to drink everything you buy the same day. You may want to store some wine for the future, and to help it remain its best, or even improve the age, the storing conditions (and your choice of wine) must really be right.

Wine benefits from a quite quiet and undisturbed life and the places you choose to keep it should be cool with a fairly even temperature, and away from direct light or sun. Bottles should always be stored on their side so that the cork remains in contact with the wine. If the cork dries out, it lets in air and the wine is spoilt (corked).

Wine racks, are of course, specially designed for the job, but you can use equally well a cardboard carton with dividers for bottles, or simply lie the bottles on their side.

Storing Wine

Wine in bottles with corks may be stored. For high quality wines, it is best to find out from the shop the ideal storing period. For wines of more modest quality, the time should be six months to a year.

Bottle, Carafe or Box

First, the right choice of wine to keep. Wine now comes in a variety of containers. As well as the traditional bottle with a cork, there are for instance, the carafe, the plastic re-sealable bottle, the can, the cardboard carton and the box; but only the bottle with a cork is actually suitable for keeping and ageing wine. Wine in all other containers is at its best drunk shortly after it is bought. The box, of course, is specially designed to keep wine fresh for a time after it has been opened, dispensing wine by the glass on tap, but the wine will not remain at its best indefinitely, and it is wise to drink it within a couple of months of purchase.

Once a bottle, carafe or carton has been opened, it would ideally have to be finished the same day. Too much exposure to air badly affects wine – but it can still be used to add to appropriate dishes for cooking. To keep left over wine fresh for a further day or two, transfer into a clean half bottle and reseal to eliminate as much air as you can.

In the case of quality sparkling wines, it is really best to drink these on the day...who wants to leave any for tomorrow anyway!!

A Practical Guide to Tasting

I can't feel it necessary to explain to anyone how to drink wine, however, 'tasting' to see all's well is another matter.

There are wine-knows who regard tasting as an art, sniffing, swirling and then pontificating at length in flowery language, and using amazing terms such as 'shy', 'frumpish', 'buxom', and I read recently, 'Tastes like wet flagstones after a shower'. Taste is such a personal thing, and as with food, it does seem rather churlish to scorn anything others like, so form your own opinions and make either a mental note or write your thoughts down – there is no need for pretentious quotes. Terms such as clean, fruity, full and dry, well balanced or full bodied are used when describing the flavour. In fact, if you wish to be serious about this, you could easily make out a pad, much as students use, something like this:

Wine

Shipper

CLARITY: Cloudy/Clear/Brilliant   **Price**

               1.2

COLOUR: Faulty/Mediocre/Typical
Colour   1.2.3

NOSE: Unclean/Neutral/Light/Fragrant/Full
Fruit aroma   1.2.3.4.5
Bouquet

PALATE: Unclean/Faulty/Balanced/
Sweetness   Typical/Outstanding 1.2.3.4.5.
Tannin   6.7.8.9.10
Acidity
Body
Balance

CONCLUSIONS: _____
Overall
Quality
Date:
      Points
         /20

If you are really serious about wine tasting, two books that you will find most helpful are;

Masterglass by Jancis Robinson (Pan Books). This is a practical course in developing tasting skills, Jancis suggests you practice spitting in the bath!

Wine's Company by Pamela Vandyke Price (Foulsham) will be useful when conducting tastings with friends. It is a practical feet-on-the-ground course which should give you many evenings of pleasurable instruction.

Tasting does have a practical aim, so don't cringe when the wine waiter hovers over you in your favourite restaurant. The reasons are:

- To estimate the quality of the wine, young or old
- Examine the general balance and condition
- To judge the state of maturity, stability and development

Points to Watch

Taste the wine in the most suitable order: dry before sweet, young before old, cheap before expensive. It is a matter of personal preference whether you try red before white, or white before red, although some experts, 'wine-knows' , would come down on the side of dry white before red.

Select your glass – ideally, short stem, rounded base, narrower end.

Swirl the wine in the glass and:

Look at the wine carefully, the eye will record clarity, haziness and deposit and of course colour.

Smell, the nose will record bouquet, fruit, flowers, spices, fragrance and so on.

Taste, the palate will record alcoholic strength from the pricking on the gums, acidity, sweetness and tannin from the tongue. Swirl the wine around the tongue and form your impressions.

Finish, the taste experienced shortly after tasting fine quality wines will stay in your memory, much like a memorable meal, and it is necessary to call on your memory when buying wine in order to price it, in an off-licence, restaurant or even auction – to decide which wines will give you best value for money, and whether to buy at the price offered.

Signs of Trouble

Travel Sickness

Like most human beings, wine needs to rest after a journey, whilst it doesn't exactly suffer from jet-lag, it doesn't enjoy being jerked around during travel or subjected to sudden changes of temperature. It is quite possible, due to faulty containers, for the wine to contract some sickness which results in the wine developing a 'musty' taste. Faults such as these can be diagnosed and when rested and cured is perfectly acceptable.

If a wine is hazy, dull or has an unnatural colour, the chances are you won't even wish to put it in your mouth, and will tread carefully. It is not often that the need to return a bottle of wine arises, but you can bet your life it will be the one occasion you most wish for everything to run smoothly, probably entertaining the boss or future in-laws. In a restaurant the waiter will present you with an ordered bottle, for you to check it is the one listed, included vintage, supplier or shipper. If it isn't it is quite possible the waiter, if he knows his stuff, has provided you with a similar wine as an alternative, should he have run out of your first choice. It is entirely up to you whether you wish to try this. If the cost is the same and you keep an open mind it

All shook up!

will probably be acceptable. The waiter will naturally provide you with a taste. Ask yourself, does the wine look, smell and taste healthy.

Young wine looks fresh in colour – even the cheapest wine should look 'alive' and not cloudy and of unnatural colour. White wines may turn gold from pale yellow. Depending on where they are made red wines start by looking light or dark purple, with age an old red wine can change to the colour of dark mahogany. Does it smell healthy, not of worn socks after a squash match, stale dish cloths, cabbage water, or rotten eggs. A sick wine can taste of any of these, any real stink means that the bottle should be rejected. A tainted glass can also cause problems, the most usual being from a glass having been placed down on a painted surface or a dirty tea towel. A wine should have a fresh, clean moderately agreeable smell. If the wine has a chemical smell it may benefit from a little air, as does the wine with no smell, swirl it around in the glass, leave it for a few moments and then sniff again. A wine that is corked is not pleasant, although it won't always taste of cork. In general, if a wine has an acrid, harsh chemical smell all is not well and you may wish to reject it, not an easy exercise but simply explain to the waiter that the wine is not as it should be, and an alternative will quickly be found.

Less difficult is to discover problems with your wine in your own home.

I don't mean to make you nervous, problems are rare. Return the defective bottle to your source of supply explaining why as soon as possible, and I'm sure your supplier will credit you immediately.

What with What

Apart from the enjoyment of wines, another of life's great pleasures must be food. A glass of the right wine will certainly enhance certain dishes. The question is, what is the right wine? Quite simply in the long run, the best combination is that which pleases with you. Everyone who enjoys a glass of wine probably has his or her own favourites when it comes to matching the bottle with the dish. There really are no unbreakable rules, and a little experimenting is always enjoyable. It would in fact, be easier to list those wines which *cannot* be served throughout a meal than the reverse. Generally speaking, the richer the food the more robust should be the wine served with it.

There are other considerations:

Awareness of cost, inability to please everybody, availability of certain wines, knowledge of temperatures, when to open the bottle, decanting, it is a wonder we find the right balance, but we do. As in many things, practice, memory and previous mistakes make perfect, it is the only way to learn. Know your guests – it's a horrible feeling to serve a Chablis-Grand Cru, to then discover your guest has a sweet tooth.

Age and year also bear consideration. Quite often wine merchants produce small cards showing the tables of 'good' and 'bad' years in the various wine regions. You can always spot the up and coming wine-know when he produces one of these cards when selecting his wines. Bear in mind two vineyards are never alike. Though from the same 'area' but separated by a fold in the hills or by a strip of forest, one has had a hailstorm setting it back for weeks or a shower of rain, whilst the other remained parched. All these factors would naturally alther the wines' characteristics. It is, therefore, useful to bear this in mind and use the cards with discretion – as a useful guideline, but only really your palate can be the decider for you.

Like menu-planning you and your guests tastes are individual. As with food it is a good idea to do some 'prep' in advance as to which wine to serve with which dishes. Avoid, if possible, clashes or repetition, i.e. Mosel followed by a Piesporter.

An Aperitif

Something light and attractive. There is no doubt a pint of Guinness would be delicious, but it would not do a great deal for your appetite. Maybe a sherry, a light wine and possibly a 'Kir' using a measure of Crème de Cassis, topped with a dry chilled white wine or sparkling wine (Kir Royale).

A cocktail or even a glass of Beaujolais Nouveau – when available – is also an idea. Try also the 'Blush' wines. Light and fruity, these delicate 'pink' wines would make good aperitifs. (see California)

Soups, Clear, Consommé, Oxtail

A dry or medium sherry though not so fashionable nowadays might be nice to try. With hearty more filling soups a Vin de Pay can fit the bill, although it is nice, if well made, to just enjoy the flavour of your soup!

Fish

The world is your oyster – dry, medium dry white wines ranging from the Muscadets and Chablis (fine with oysters and other shellfish) through to Piesporter and Orvieto. The choice greatly depends on the method of cooking and the sauce served.

White Meats

Most German wines accompany chicken and veal well, but nothing is better with a Coq au Vin (chicken in wine) than a glass of fresh young Beaujolais, a typical example of the sauce indicating the appropriate wine to serve.

Red Meats

Really good red wines make splendid partners for plainly roasted joints. Depending on your preference possibly a Burgundy to accompany a rare roast beef, a red Bordeaux (Claret) or the Californian Cabernets would be a good choice for a succulent roasted leg of lamb. For casseroles, stews and pies the weighty full wines could be your choice, possibly a Rhône or a Spanish red. The Wine Development Board's red wine taste chart could help you here.

Game

Strong full bodied wines, like a good Rhône, try Châteauneuf du Pape, a Spanish Rioja or maybe an Italian Barolo or the less hefty Barbaresco.

Cheese

Really an enjoyable way to finish the last of the red wine – it is understandable to see why the French make this their penultimate course. A glass of good Port would also be a treat.

Sweets

Depending on the lightness of the dish, most medium sweet and sweet white wines would be suitable. A good Asti Spumante is at times very good with sweet dishes. It is open for discussion, but it is said any sweet containing more than 30 per cent chocolate does not require a wine.

Fruit and Nuts

Brown Sherry, Sweet Madeira or Marsala are all worthy of consideration, but Port is said to be drunk with nuts, frankly I'll drink port with anyone!

Coffee

Liqueurs, – as with wines the choice is wide.

A glass of port, or a cognac to aid digestion would put the finishing touches on the meal.

Note: A range of champagnes would complement all dishes within a meal. It would certainly get the party going as an aperitif.

17 *Learning More*

Suggested Reading and Useful Addresses

For all 'wine-knows' who are fast becoming 'hooked' on the subject here are some ways to further your knowledge.

Books on the subject, just a few you may find helpful:

Pocket Book of Winetasting Michael Broadbent (Mitchell Beazley)
The Penguin Wine Book Pamela Vandyke Price (Penguin)
The Great Wine Book Jancis Robinson (Sidgwick & Jackson)
Encyclopedia of Wines and Spirits Alexis Lichines (Cassell)
Wine, World Atlas of Wine and *Pocket Wine Book* Hugh Johnson (Mitchell Beazley)
The Wine Lover's Guide to France Michael Busselle (Michael Joseph)

I could go on forever, the list is endless, other excellent wine writers to look out for are, husband and wife team David Peppercorn, and Serena Sutcliff. Steven Spurrier is yet another excellent authority, and a personal favourite of mine, *Sunday Telegraph* wine correspondent, Robert Joseph.

Still on reading, the Wine Guides *Websters* and *Which Wine Guide* will be very useful when selecting and finding good value for money.

148

There are, of course, several monthly publications:

Decanter Magazine, 2 - 10 St Johns Road, London SW11 1PN
Wine, 55 Heath Road, Twickenham, Middlesex, TW1 4AW
Also *Which Wine Monthly* from the Consumers' Assocation, Castlemead, Gascoyne Way, Hetford SG14 1LH

These magazines provide up-to-date snippets of information, and will include 'Wine Diaries' with dates of tutored wine tastings and courses in your area, or even out of your area – what better excuse for a jolly weekend away?

The Wine Development Board whom I gratefully acknowledge for their help with providing information for this book are another good source for any general enquires you may have: 5 Kings House, Kennet Wharf Lane, Upper Thames Street, London EC4U 3BH.

The Wine and Spirit Education Trust run lectures and courses all over the country. They have two useful self-help study guides for students, *The New Wine Companion* and *Wine Regions of the World* by David Burroughs and Norman Bezzant. I have found both extremely helpful.

Last but not least probably the best and most pleasurable way to further your knowledge is of course – *drink it* – wine bars all over the country enable you to try several different wines without purchasing a whole bottle. Enjoy yourself, but leave the car keys at home. All the other ways I'm sure you know – I just hope this book has been of some help to you when making your purchase, at whatever source suits the event. your convenience and importantly, your pocket!